EXOTIC EPIPHANIES

Published in the United States by
Beckham Publications Group, Inc.
P.O. Box 4066, Silver Spring, MD 20914

ISBN: 978098334029-4

Library of Congress Cataloging in Publication:

Exotic Epiphanies

Elinor Floum

PREFACE

I was beginning, wondering how to juggle a life of travel and the arduous requirements of a graduate psychoanalytic institute.

My efforts to stay afloat—even to master these conflicting endeavors – to study, stay married, travel, see patients, undergo an intense personal psychoanalysis, stay on speaking terms with my kids; in short to have some fun and not go nuts is the genesis of this offering.

It contains a rather fragmented, impressionistic picture of places, events and states of mind, from silly through sad and somber (and nuances in between), that reflects my desire to share, to disclose myself—to be known. I fear to have been too open; I hope not to be harshly judged; and I trust there will be that which might amuse as well as touch the reader.

TABLE OF CONTENTS

HOME

That's how it was here—all mail neatly stowed in a giant basket, newspapers all stacked in my office halfway to the ceiling after two months. I've decided not to try to catch up on the story line of Mary Worth, and they carried Dr. Rex Morgan in the International Edition of the *London Herald Tribune*, so I'll just carry on there.

The rooms I thought I liked the best—I don't The living room, which was decorated 12 years ago, and I thought I was tired of—I love. Of course it's English chintzes, beiges, rusts, navy blues, and English antiques on coffee-with-cream-coloured carpets. Of course I love it—it's like home.

But such an antiseptic feeling. Hubby went to sleep early and I was *afraid* to unpack! To make the first billow of trashing of this pristine environment with dirty clothes, souvenirs, do-dads, etc. Thank goodness I woke up to a general blitzkrieg as Hubby had opened the mail and stacks and piles were sitting around everywhere all over again. Home—my home again. Not Jimmy's—the super neat lawyer who house-sat for us for two months. Or Sara, our housekeeper, who loves everything her way, neat and unread, unplayed-with, uncluttered. I love it that way too. But then I'd have to move in elsewhere and mark my turf with all my comforting little droppings. I even have relaxed and regrouped enough to have books, notebook, pen and letters back in bed with me.

There's a lovely note from number one son who was fairly snarkey before he left for his trip but is sweet, as usual, at a distance. This distance was a good one—we in London, he in Nepal, for two months.

Number two son over yesterday, calm, cheery, living his own life. Growing up. Going to try to get this house together. I guess I mean internal as well as external, but I'm thinking of external environment. Blue rug in office to office bathroom stained unacceptably by traffic. I've tried to ignore it but can't. A thousand things need repairing and decisions. To spend money, that is, or not. With most rooms I'd have to start all over. With my life, too. And my body. And my career. How come just as we get a little smart and experienced—it's time to decompose?

A SMALL FAMILY HISTORY: JUST THE OVERVIEW, MA'AM — THE PSYCHOLOGICAL STUDIES WILL TAKE LONGER

To my children and grandchildren, as time passes, it becomes more and more hard to remember and trace past events, so I want to tell you a story about your forebears. I wish I knew more about my own.

In the days of large waves of Jewish immigration from Russia, 1906-07, my mother's father Robert Levine escaped from pogroms and Cossacks by fleeing from the Port of Odessa to America. On the boat coming over, in steerage no doubt, he met a pretty woman named Rose. After they cleared Ellis Island and Robert found work, perhaps in a furniture company or factory, Robert and Rose were married, My mother Anna Levine, was born in Indianapolis, Indiana where Robert had gone to pursue work in a furniture mill. The family subsequently moved back to New York City, no doubt to be near his four sisters. I remember them well, mostly and at first because of their names... Sonia, Tanya, Brauna and Lisa. By the time I was coming in from Williamsport, Pa. to visit my mother's sister, Aunt Lil, they were animated old ladies living in a huge apartment on the Riverside Drive, crocheting patterned blankets and contradicting each other. Aunt Lisa made me a patterned bedspread which has gotten lost in the many moves since.

The whole family was eager to assimilate, in those days they came from much violence toward Jews in Russia, where they were persecuted and/or conscripted into the Czar's army (see *Fiddler on the Roof*). My grandfather and the sisters were ardent students of the language, a11 wrote and spoke English very well and never stopped studying and enjoying their adopted language. Grandfather Robert, after whom Josh was second-named, had a letter to the editor published in the *New York Times*, and was very proud of that. No one wanted to be a "greenhorn." That meant fresh off the boat, with babushka and peasant clothing.

No one was more eager to be hip and with it than some of these immigrants, many went into the garment industry and dressed as well as they possibly could—sticking out and being different were anathema. My mother's family early learned about and found apparel outlets, factory seconds, and clothes were a hot item of discovery and enjoyment. My grandfather spouted Marxism. He believed in its tenets, and espoused the philosophy. Religion, he often stated, was the opiate of the people, whenever anyone talked about God or things spiritual, he would laugh and say, "aach, such foolishness."

His son Melvin's son Roger, (my first cousin Roger Levin) is observant; and that reminds me, I must ask him what happened to the final E. on the Levine name. Is it better to cut that off?

Also, Grandpa Robert turned himself into a very tidy little capitalist. He took an obvious flair for machines and opened a cash register business in the Bronx, just off the Grand Concourse. After Uncle Mel's stint in the Coast Guard, he worked with his father in the business, repairing, selling, and delivering registers to local businesses. I remember being in the store, and that upon meeting and parting, Grandpa and Uncle Mel would kiss each other on both cheeks and hug enthusiastically. I always loved seeing that, more French style than Waspy American homophobic style. Come to think of it, show business folk do that, and we all know many of them were Jewish immigrants—not least second generation— originally.

Grandmother Rose died young, at 44, of a series of strokes. My grandfather married twice more. In fact, on his last honeymoon in his seventies, he and his wife were visiting the Grand Canyon in Arizona, driving with a young family they met in their hotel, when an inebriated American Indian lost control of his pickup truck and hit their automobile, killing all four adults, and only a small child in the back seat between two adults survived. Although he allegedly had some kind of heart trouble, it is remarkable that he had the energy and *joie de vivre* to try marriage again in his seventies; also he never retired and was still working in the shop with Uncle Mel when this happened.

I talk exclusively about my mother's family, why? Because, first of all, all of my other three grandparents were dead before I was born, so I never knew them. Secondly, my mother was none too fond of his family, except for his brother Phil, who still lived in Philadelphia. Also, my mother felt superior to most of them, I think. She had great social aspirations, and some of them were very unsophisticated.

My father's folks were originally from Kiev, farmers. My mother's father was a pharmacist in Odessa before he came to the United States, quite an exalted occupation for a Jew in those days. She used to talk of her Zayda, her grandfather, and I have seen pictures of him, very very tall and handsome, and evidently spoiled her silly, which naturally she loved. I must ask Roger more about him, our mutual great-grandfather.

Unfortunately in that family, there were rifts and abandonments and tons of jealousy, factions of the family quit speaking, forever and ever, to other factions. My mother had numerous cousins whom she drifted away from, so I must gather some more history while I can.

She was not interested in my father's numerous relatives, with the exception of a wealthy (and anti-Semitic) half-brother, Charles Goodman, who was raised as an orphan at Girard College in Philadelphia when his mother couldn't keep him. He got a job sweeping out the floors of a watch factory, rose through the ranks and of course ended up being president of the company—Hamilton Watch Factory—owning an apartment building as well as living in Stamford, Connecticut, while refusing to rent to Jews. How's that for assimilating? When in Connecticut, etc. do as they do. Okay. He married a tall slender non-Jewish woman, Aunt Claire. I visited one time, woke up with a ferocious beast slobbering over me. It was their boxer, and I learned they are really sweeties, but not till I almost died of fright first. So I knew two of my father's brothers. There were many more half-brothers.

Uncle Charlie was famous for being rich, and for being the only person ever to die of a jelly-fish sting, not allergic reaction. He was swimming in Florida with a doctor friend of his and died there. There was a write-up that I saw saying he had died but not of an allergic reaction. I wish now I had saved that article, of course then genealogy was not of interest to me.

Uncle Phil was very good-natured and used to call me peanut. Such a sweet guy, he however, I found out later, was a slum lord in south Philly, renting out those god-awful slum apartments.

Oh, that's right. One last encounter we had with Uncle Charlie: when we were stationed in Germany where your father Josh was born in 1958, Charlie and Claire came over to tour and to buy their Mercedes from the factory in Stuttgart. Dick and I went to Frankfurt-Am Main to meet them at the Frankfurter-Hof where we had dinner. Dick was a specialist 4th class in the army, and to say we didn't have much money was putting it mildly. Anyway, after dinner Uncle Charlie tried to figure out the tip to leave, in Deutschmarks, of course, and Dick told him what would be a good tip, a great tip, and an okay one. I will never forget my Uncle Charlie starting to sweat and shake with the decision, quite literally. Finally, he left so little that Dick went back on some pretext to the table and added some coins. So much for big-time spending in that family.

My father's family who came from Kiev did not fare as well as my mother's educated family. My paternal grandfather, according to my Dad, worked on a milk truck and on the trolley line in Philadelphia, his poor fingers froze in the winter, and my father tried to help and put medicine on to heal them. He wanted to be a doctor, it is said, but wound up going to Philadelphia College of Pharmacy for a few years, and had drugstores of his own eventually. My Dad and my mother met on the boardwalk in Atlantic City. Now, in those pre-airconditioning years, anyone who could scrape the tariff together would get to the shore for the summer since it was brutally hot and humid in the cities. New Yorkers tended to go to Coney Island by subway, and to Long Island, but Atlantic City was chock-full of Philly folks.

The lore is that my father, Louis Forman, pursued her, Anna Levine, for five years, that she was reluctant…but her mother was very ill and wanted to see my mother settled down with someone with his own business…and pressured her. At least that's her story, and it may as well be true. Her mother died three months before my older sister Rhoda was born, and my mother stayed in what was an unhappy marriage till the end of their lives. My father moved from Germantown, Philadelphia, where I was born in 1931 and where I remember the drugstore he owned, and that we lived in back of. He found an opportunity he wanted in Washington, D.C., and we moved there when I was six. When I was nine, we moved to Williamsport, Pa. where my father finally got out of that business, because, he said, he hated to get up early in the morning to open up. He was a dyed in-the-wool night-owl and pretty much hated mornings. He opened up bowling alleys, 24, opposite the Lycoming Aircraft Plant, and of course along came WWII and he prospered. I went to Curtain Grade School, Stevens Junior High School, and Williamsport High School, now Lycoming College.

After that, my parents moved to the outskirts of New York, Larchmont, where my father had more bowling alleys. That includes, always, the lunch counter and tables business. So it was bowling and a restaurant business. He spent most of his time there, and mother ran the house, so it was not a cooperative marriage, let us say. They took separate vacations and had separate friends.

From there, at 18, I went off to Penn State, a mere sixty miles away from Williamsport, but a long way from New York where the rest of the family moved. It was glorious getting away from the family and their almost constant battling, which I always hated. The dorms (Simmons) were an oasis of peace and quiet by comparison. I was a liberal arts major, and enjoyed the classes and location, if not the bitter cold winters. Brrrrr.

The next year, my sophomore one, I, Elinor Forman, was suddenly seated next to a certain ubiquitous Richard Floum. See, Forman and Floum were alphabetically next to one another. So in social sciences, history, English, all the required courses, as well as art history and drama—there he was. Sorry to say, I thought he was a big smart alec. I found out later that he was really very shy, and in an attempt to overcome that trait, he went to the opposite extreme. He was forever lecturing to me about things, giving me booklists to read and acting generally obnoxious and omnipotent. He asked me out numerous times, and I said no. And finally changed my seat away from him in all the classes we shared. The bossy know-it-all-ness covered up a very sweet person, but it took me six or seven years to find that out.

Graduation found us parading ceremonially cheek-by-tassel with one another; we even introduced the parents to one another before the ceremony, since we were all assembled together.

From there, he went to University of Pennsylvania Law School, I went to Columbia University for a master's degree in English and teaching of English. Then I student taught. Then I worked at teaching for a year. The New York kids were too tough for a 22-year-old teacher, and where I worked in New City, New York required that I live up the Hudson Valley, so I was very very isolated. I taught eighth and ninth grade English in New City, New York. So I got out of teaching and got a job writing catalogue copy for Montgomery Ward. I worked on Canal Street, way downtown, and lived uptown near Columbia University, at 103rd and Amsterdam Avenue.

One hot summer day in 1955 I squeezed myself into the subway as usual to get downtown to work, and looked up to see who I was trying not to get squished by, when lo and behold, it was Richard Floum. I asked what he doing in New York and he said that he was working on Wall Street for the summer between his second and third years of law school. He knew my folks had moved to the city, but was amazed that we both lived uptown and worked downtown. I remember it was a Monday. He said, I'll come and visit you tonight, it's a block away. I said, as usual, "No I'm tired, I'm going to wash my hair and go to bed early."

That evening, towel around my hair I answered the door, and yep, it was him. Well, he was sort of an old familiar figure, if not a friend, and we started meeting and eventually dating.

However, some of my duties were as a pre-shrink, since he had lots of troubles he wanted help with. We broke up when he moved back to Pennsylvania, then started seeing each other again around Thanksgiving.

He decided at New Year's we should get married. I was terrified, having never, literally, seen a happy marriage. My parents fought constantly, my aunt and uncle had a distant, frigid marriage, and my sister got divorced after six weeks of marriage! My sister Rhoda's husband, Chick, was moved to the sofa, then out the door, then in record time she moved back in with her parents. The thank-you notes from her wedding presents had barely cooled down and been mailed when she flounced back from Philadelphia to New York.

Okay, I figured I'd try it, give it a year. Marriage, I mean. He had grown on me, and I had discovered his sweet side. Oh yes: my father never liked anyone I dated. My mother only liked them if they had lots and lots of money. Dick didn't, he was a scholarship student. I was reluctant to have them meet Dick; but after we decided to try marriage I thought, oh well, well get the families together and if they don't like each other, so be it. We tried. We'll avoid them if they are too horrible.

Much to our surprise, they not only liked each other, but the mothers discovered that they had been in the hospital at the same time to have their babies—my birthday 8/11/31, his 8/26/31—which had been delivered by the same doctor at Philadelphia Jewish Women's Hospital. Dick always claimed after that that I had stolen his rattle, since I was older and discharged before him. In those days women were kept "confined" for two weeks after birth, if can you believe that. Humane.

I call it destiny. We had to pass, like ships in the night, three times across each other's path before we joined together in marriage. Though there were ups and downs and problems to be worked on throughout our forty-year marriage, I always loved Grandpa. Always and only. Before, during and after our marriage he was the one and only man I ever seriously loved and the only one I ever envisioned marrying. Indeed, we both worked on the marriage and ourselves, sometimes reluctantly on his part but he always responded to my ultimatums about getting help or else. And he said it was the best thing that ever happened to him, the getting of help.

So that, dear kiddies, is the story of how, astronomically, alphabetically and geographically your parents, grandparents and great-grandparents (in the case of Jessica and Jackson) have met and married.

To be continued.

GRADUATION

The big day came, at last. Dane's graduation from law school and a culmination devoutly wished for and enjoyed. He was free of classes and grades! Hurray to us both. This one had not gone straight to his target, no sir, Bob. He thought about it while doing many projects and things, environmentally correct, was demographically minded, ecologically hip and worked hard to save Mono Lake.

Now, aha, our do-gooder was going to put that nose to the grindstone like the rest of us, and *sacre bleu*! Join the middle class, (wherever it might be).

Hubby and I would have walked, swum, crawled up to San Francisco to be at that ceremony at the Civic Center Auditorium, let alone driven up in our new car. (We got manic with joy on the way back, and returned by way of Highway One, going south yet, that means being on the crumbling cliff-side of a most scenic, but nauseatingly curvy road looking down toward rocks and cliffs past the crumbling edge of the road. Whew. Anyway, as I said, I would have taken a moose-ride through Saskatchewan, a camel-ride in Egypt, or a kayak in Kenya to be at this much-anticipated graduation.

It was a glorious, if cold and windy day. After the event, we had drinks, dinner, and then back to his place for a celebratory concert. He played and sang, and the rest of us joined him, for the best song-fest we ever had. Everyone was in fine spirits and even better voice.

We eagerly awaited the return of the film of the events, not only as a memento of this superb evening, but also for the folks back East who could not make it out to the graduation, for reasons of health and fitness.

Precautions had been taken for a goof-proof set of pictures. I had had my Nikon serviced, loaded up with film, extra film and fresh batteries were at the ready. There was a professional photographer taking pictures as each candidate was hooded with the magical cowl that signified the much-desired degree of *juris doctor*, and if that were not enough, a girlfriend had her camera with her, and Josh, our older son, had received a brand new Pentax that day for his birthday. It could be said we were covered.

Not really. That night, Josh's camera stopped working. My Nikon wouldn't close after the first roll was loaded. We received our check for $52.50 back from the film company, who claimed they had never heard of us or the Hastings Law School Graduation! A single roll of film Josh had taken and given us before we left, besides having the ruined pictures, had a few dark, blurred images of the festivities, in which Dane could be made out, if one had eagle vision, ESP, and an excellent imagination. Tuesday I will call the photo crew and plead for sanity and some pics, but meantime my mother and sister might have to be content with what we have in hand. The president of the law school is draping the cowl around someone who could just as well be Yogi Barra, Yitzhak Rabin or Yma Sumac, (but really it was Alex Floum) for all the clarity we can muster. Oh boy, what a waste of time!

The school promised in a brochure that the event would be videotaped for our future pleasure; I didn't see any tapes, but I will pursue that as well. Doctor Dane is now studying for the bar and cannot be asked to pursue any other business at the moment. Well hope for the best, but oh those awful pictures, in 5 by 7 size yet. As the kids say, you had to be there. And have a mighty good memory.

AS THE SONG GOES...

As the song goes, I know a little bit, about a lot of things, but I don't know enough about..sports fans. Oh I know that men, usually, get very carried away with their teams as some sort of expression of male bonding. As a professional observer of our species I want to investigate less obvious meanings. It's not an academic question; I've recently come through a harrowing Lakers' season, and I cannot say my nerves will ever be the same.

Let me put it this way: I like the Lakers. I like them a lot. They are my home team. They are my neighbors. I see a lot of them in my daily rounds and at the gas station or at the Good Earth having breakfast, walking down Westwood Boulevard. Having reunions at the Century Plaza Hotel.

My son has been a basketball aficionado since first grade; he takes after his dad that way. As he grew older he used to quiz me on the Lakers team and their season averages. Team pictures occupied the place of honor in his bedroom.

So why am I so puzzled now? Well, older son has been away from home a good while. He happened to be in town this last weekend of the playoffs, and the maelstrom of emotion emanating from the TV room was so intense I got quite worried. It seemed both my husband and my son were in the midst of a severe mental decompensation.

Rooting for the home team is one thing, but I tell you the air was blue with expletives, groans, screams, shrieks of terror and howls of rage I haven't seen the likes of since the whole family went to see the *Exorcist*, and of course, lived to regret it. Older son wasn't the same after that, the whole family was a bit shaky actually. The affect during this playoff was more agonized than if we had sat through a triple bill of *Alien, Poltergeist*, and a chainsaw movie all rolled up in one...not a pretty picture.

I am not unsophisticated about issues of projective identification. I know in theory that the person makes the prowess of the team his personal prowess. That this is a random universe and it is taken as a signifier that if your team is a winner, then you are too. I realize all of that. But the violence of this identification startles me profoundly, I must admit. The total absorption, the loss of reality and awareness that it is not actually happening to him chills me not a little. What is at stake here anyway? Nothing much I can identify with, that's the thing. Sure, it would be nice if they won. No one will vote against his own home team. And there's not even money in it. Only ego, power and pride.

My husband says I need a shot of testosterone to understand this. Maybe so, but I notice lots of young women are getting into it. Maybe the sense of having to compete for every scrap of food and foothold in the world is spreading finally.

As for me, if I am not a team mother, wife, manager or stockholder, I cannot see being that vitally involved. I don't think I have the intestinal fortitude to care about the things I need to care about and still have all that steam for the Lakers.

Maybe that's the point: with the biosphere evaporating from holes in the ozone layer and pesticides building up in our fatty tissues and HIV viruses floating around blood banks, we need something safe to go crazy over, where the consequences will not be as fatal. Maybe basketball is a transference object for battles of a much more perilous nature.

Okay, Sigmund Freud would call it substitution. Maybe displacement…of non-vital concerns for the real life fears of not being able to make a living, feed your family, remain safe and intact against hostile others or a hostile environment. That year of studying old Sigmund has come in handy after all. Cancel my appointment with the Dalai Lama, I don't need the trip to Tibet after all.

MADE IN HEAVEN

How H. and I ever got together—let alone stay together—is, frankly speaking, beyond me! We have different tastes in practically everything but the major ones—each other, kids, home.

In literature, we both love it—but not the same kinds. Chances are if I hate it, he'll love it and vice-versa, including this little contribution to the arts.

He loves spectator sports—and I don't. Ditto playing basketball, bridge, shell collecting and detective stories.

I love things having to do with relationships, children, dogs, cats and Erica Jong. He doesn't. Ditto long talks on the phone with friends, gossip—which of course as an analyst-in-training I am trying to exorcise from my repertoire of behavior.

I used to love dancing but I haven't done it in so long my glass slippers have turned into Dr. Hisses and need built-in arch supports! And, my lumbago has lumbered its last bago years and years ago.

We have, mutually, to raise our heads to see each other clearly through our his and hers bifocals.

And, I've slipped from a "Miss Bonwit" many long blocks downtown to "Miss Lane Bryant Chubettes" before settling at, frankly, "Matrons and/or Mothers."

I like sitcoms about families—he doesn't. He doesn't even like Bill Cosby! I also like lectures about Freud, object relations and the death instinct. He would rather get on a bus to Cucamonga or go to the dentist for a week. I love gardens and pet shows and open houses; he likes war movies and anything with Nazis in it. I love shopping malls and new department stores; he would rather mop the bathroom floor. I particularly love new babies and infants of every description, plus their little outfits and accoutrements; he's bored 'til they can throw a basketball back.

But Thank God—we both love the beach, Fiji and our kids. And, each other. What more do you want from a fifties marriage that has survived 'til the eighties?!? He loves puzzles, logic games and legal principles. Ditto eggplant parmesan. I hate puzzles, can't do any of these things—and the eggplant dish for which he is famous all over the west side gives me the pip. I adore kittens, Elizabeth Taylor and doctor shows, which make him sneeze a lot.

(Do you think this match was made in heaven??)

Ditto shopping for clothes, looking at jewelry, and trying on new lipsticks. Worst of all, he's retiring for the night with a mystery story or shoot-em-up while I am just getting ready to concentrate on some studying or writing. The man has *never* made it to *Hill Street Blues*, let alone Johnny Carson.

I'm good 'til 1:30 or 2:00 a.m. Needless to say, we do not interface at breakfast. (My face is still on my pillow.)

Fortunately, we are equally allergic to *some* relatives, staying with people in their homes, and camping. And we love our children, tropical islands, and many other things, but most of all—each other.

I'm happy to say that I caught the second airing of the MTV awards, Channel 28 kindly re-aired the special. I hate missing a big media event like this; it was a cultural phenomenon. And a truly terrifying insight into young people today—their loves, their hates, their taste. What makes them tick?

Maybe Dr. Spock and his generation of raise-em-by-the-book babies was a bust, maybe far, far more permissiveness was needed than even that gray eminence advised. Here's why. If that lot was not the most rebellious of humanoids ever seen. Their clothes give new meaning to "way far out." Now, it's true that every generation thinks its young people are more depraved, disobedient and sacreligious than any other. And maybe they're right.

Everyone from Euripides, a Greek playwright of the fifth century before Christ, for heaven's sake, to sages of the Muslim and Buddhist worlds have exhorted young people to follow the moral course and not to give their elders *tsoursis*. But, honestly, even Victorian rakes, among the most degenerate of folks, at the least dressed beautifully, in fact were dandies. Even by the standards of other people. (Of course, these MTV'ers spend untold time and money looking raunchy; perhaps they are appreciated by their peers.

Caligula's court didn't really specialize in wholesome, but they at least pressed their togas and combed their hair. Jewels and snazzy scents, foods and cosmetic emollients were not unknown to the ancients.

Sartorially speaking, these TV doings (shall we call them dontings?) were a disaster, belonging right up there on the wall of *Naked Gun 2 and 1/2*....remember where they pictured the Titanic sinking, the Hindenburg falling....Michael Dukakis?

Did entertainers ever before get onstage wearing stripes, plaids and polka dots all in one outfit? And shredded pants. My younger son looked like that going out the door to nursery school and kindergarten. In addition his buttons were often mis-buttoned. Did I scold and rail? No, I let him be, figuring his peer group would clue him about threads they liked and those they didn't. It did, now he is the second most fastidious dresser in the family, could give Ivy League lessons to Brooks Brothers salesmen.

I figure the gang on MTV must have either come from the Baptist Belt or fresh over the wall of the convent, to be so raring to break any and all taboos. Or they had relatives like Huckleberry Finn's darling, but strict Aunt Emily, who fussed for hours at an infraction of etiquette.

Those small screen idols are by far the most embarrassing group. Did you catch Prince's er....contribution? There's no rebuttal like his rebuttal... Clothes courtesy of Sodom and Gomorrah? Oh that's right, good taste is out. The ambiance was generally degenerate, I'm afraid we're bringing a new wave of fundamentalism down upon ourselves wily-nilly. I'm sort of surprised the mullahs and ayatollahs and our good Brother Yusuf (formally the ultra-cool Cat Stevens) have not put a price on the heads of the producers, directors and cast of this shindig altogether.

Rampant general bad taste, but specific outrageousness form Prince, taking a page out of Madonna's soiled book of infamy. Madonna: You and Zsa Zsa are neck in neck for the most disgusting female wanna-be entertainers in the country today. Prince: go hang out your heinie somewhere else. It's not cute when Roseanne and Tom do it, it's not cute when you do it even though your tushie may be smaller and *cafe au lait.*

MARRIED TO THE LAW

I'm wondering if there aren't certain shades of experience those of us married to lawyers share, which are unknown to others traveling in less legalistic circles. Just as criminals have their argot, shrinks their psychobabble (which hubbly detest, natch), docs their lingo… lawyers are replete with specialized Latinate terminology, initials and mindset, inbred, in the case of our family, for generations. These barristers use more initials than the F.B.I., C.I.A., and F.A.A all rolled up together. Sometimes when their legal breezes blow hard (90 m.p.h., with gusts up to 120), I hardly recognize our beloved native tongue; is this English or Esperanto? Furthermore, to get quite personal, not only my father-in-law and husband, but both sons and their girlfriends are lawyers—litigators, to be exact. That leaves me, the lone civilian and a shrink to boot, snowed in blizzard of O.S.C.'s, T.R.O.'s, and L.B.O.'s, incorporeal hereditaments, mere usufructs, collateral estoppels, and I don't know what alls.

Every family dinner is a debate between those who agree with the Clayton Act, Section 7, and those who prefer the Sherman Anti-Trust angle. I myself care not a fig, either way is fine, I just like to admire my family members flushed with the excitement of the debate, and think hmmm, this one's got dimples, and that one's got green eyes, and they all have great smiles! I'll settle for *habeus HANDSOME corpus*, Learned Hand, Abe Fortas and Clarence Darrow notwithstanding. (The world may be trying to liberate me, but all I want to do is stand around and "glow in plaid," as they say in Hollywood.)

Besides arguing about the law, "the kids" love to argue about teams and sports, the girls being more rabid fans even than crazed males…guess that goes with the territory of being competitive to the max.

Trips to Europe are piquant with a lawyer, as well. When visiting the Uffizi Gallery in Florence, we marvel at the "statutes." At the pastry shops in Germany, we indulge in rich delicious "torts." Hubby is unable to remember the civilian version of those similar sounding words of the trade.

And just as he would rather walk across burning coals than listen to a patient telling him about her depression, I have been known to log plenty of z's while observing Hubby in the courtroom. I've suffered, from time to time, from bouts with insomnia, but get me into one of those Department 4 courtrooms, particularly in Bakersfield, where Hubby is very prone toward accepting cases and practicing law, and I nod off in about eight seconds, flat. Last week I got there, and Hubby began to produce "documents" to shore up his argument that his poor schlub of a client was not siphoning off funds from a family trust, but rather had all the right in the world to doctor up the books for a score of reasons. You do know, don't you, that lawyers are not supposed to search for the "truth," preach what is right, wrong, culpable or heroic. They are simply supposed to convince. Don't you know they represent their client's point of view, regardless of their own feelings, beliefs or intuitions? Well, true to code, Hubby was holding forth enthusiastically up onto a huge screen, all the miserable records of endless dreary transactions, going through them line by line for maximum cumulative effect… no laggard, he. I didn't like it, couldn't understand it, and wouldn't believe it if I could do any of the above.

So, pretty soon my head was waving around, and was gently snoring, right there in Department 4 in front of all the jurors, plus the hostile side of the spectator seating, glaring at me. Hubby was amused. I woke with a start and was mortified. I was there, ostensibly, to provide the atmosphere of loyal wife to righteous lawyer and "good guy" clients; as opposed to the bad guy side who had only two malevolent relatives glowering on the distaff, or left side of the room. It reminded me of nothing so much as the parties at the shotgun wedding sizing each other up… that or the witnesses at a lynching party. God, I pitied those jurors. How they kept their sanity when each side planned to drone on for two or three months more, was beyond me. I hoped they were getting hardship pay…if this was American justice, it sure was long-winded… you need the patience of a saint to care all that much about any of these characters. One wondered if their mother and lawyers truly could.

Now lawyers are smooth, and lawyers are slick, but lawyers, my dears, are most of all bought. And another dirty secret I'll share: they like each other a lot better than they like any of their clients. When all of the dust and smoke settles and clears, they will meet again in another courtroom, and maybe switch sides, have a good laugh, or arrange to "do" lunch. It's a game you see, and they have lots more in common with other players of the game than with their sometimes hapless clients.

Lots of it is psycho drama; the injured parties are carefully costumed and coached to send a certain message (proud, honest, upstanding, earnest, wholesome). Relatives ditto, to impress judge and jury.

But all this is "moot" and immaterial: we Americans feel that twelve honest people can make heads or tails out of technical issues so dense it would stun the brain of a Delphic oracle.

I hear about the case behind the scenes, and I can scarcely "grok" it, even knowing the real skinny. How are these folks, many of whom are not Phi Beta Kappas from Yale, to sort through the maze of detailed data, specific to professions they do not practice? I dunno. So far I have managed to avoid jury duty; I feel I've done my bit for our American way of life at home, where the *corpus delecti* is hidden, and *res judicata* still reigns.

Sort of socially anti-social. Eventually everyone drifted home, having gotten plastered, broken glassware and blown horns for hours.

Today, January 1st, tons of garbage festoon the Sydney, Australia concert hall plaza till about 11a.m., when the very well paid garbage crews, unioned to a fare-thee-well and making at least time and a half, hauled it happily away. The seagulls all have stomach aches, but it was a wonderful, rather Dickensonian blast of old time barbarism that's best left as it is. When the populace can go conveniently ape once a year, it's a lot better that they do it then, and sober up in a timely way. Be good citizens all year long, then have next year to look forward to bottle-bashing and fandangoing again. Organized disintegration, every society allows for it whether you call it Mardi Gras, Octoberfest, fasching, or … all peoples have feast or orgy days (if not communally and periodically, the people will do it privately and constantly.)

On January 1st of almost every year, I meditate on the fresh start one has in a fresh year. Almost anything can happen this year. But I always, almost ineluctably, must muse on there being no miracles.... Because if there were, lots and lots of people would awaken January 1st being HALF AS FAT, but twice as sweet, smart, svelte, slim, supple, sophisticated, strong, scintillating, serene, sinewy, sincere, science-minded... so on. Not to mention healthier, younger, yes, younger. In fact, TWO times younger. Does that mean half as old? Hmm... so much for prayers and magic.

If Australia had more water inland it would be Shangra-la indeed.

LAW COURTS AND LOCAL CONSTABULARY

When we travel, we love to check up on, and to think about, two sets of local phenomena, as being particularly revealing of a country. They are the court system and the police–and attitudes toward the police.

We've had fascinating visits with magistrates in Vancouver, bewigged, gowned and often sitting under portraits of Queen Elizabeth, while lady lawyers back out of the courtroom, curtseying before the final fade away. Gives one a hint about what really underlies some basic concepts of their schools, churches, organizations. A conservative, old-fashioned kind of value system in Canada, I can assure you.

In Singapore, we were not aware of the huge Indian presence until a visit to the courthouse. There, judges and both sets of lawyers were Indian. All the high-level legal positions seem to be captured by Indians; they really are the Jews of the East, aren't they?

It was a different story in Suva, capita of Fiji. In Fiji, although many Indians have risen to the shop keepers estate, they originally were brought over to work the *copra plantaions*. They've retained their dress, customs and prejudices. One of the main ones seems to be against the easy-going, party-loving Polynesians.

It seems that all the folks pressing charges were Indian, all the malefactors were Polynesians. Whooping it up, and occasionally swiping a sari off someone's clothesline were the indictments; the judge doubled for the young magistrate portrayed in *Passage to India.* The one in Suva was similarly upper class, accentuated British; patiently tending to a variety of accusations that sounded more appropriate to the ministrations of the principal of Beverly Hills High than to adults in a working society. Pushing, shoving, smacking were mentioned.

The ancient courthouse building in the middle of crowded, torrid Suva was dusty and heavily weathered, the little courtrooms were overcrowded, with families either of the accused or the accusing (the former flowing aggrievedly out into the hallways.) The magistrate counseled one and all to forgive, make-up, "reconcile." He advised most defendants to keep their hands in their pockets when passing his neighbor's clothes line; this advice had to be translated through the several translators. Most of the factions did not speak each other's patois. Most Indians apparently do not speak Polynesian, which does not endear them to their host country. There were many hurt feelings, much cutting up and giggling by the gallery of on-lookers, many pow-wows to ponder settlement offers.

The judge persuaded the reluctant lady to accept $5.00 Fijian as restitution for her sari, which had been purloined by said defendant from its clothesline that separated their domiciles. And furthermore, he was to promise to keep his hands to himself and never ever to bother this lady again; ditto her property. He smiled, shrugged some more, and looked repentant not at all. Would she deign to accept this, plus his public chastisement? No response for a very long time. The judge repeated his question several times more. She finally gave a tiny nod, yes. The defendant is jubilant. His friends laugh and hug each other. Reconciliation.

I hope the Fijians can hang on to their holding: they are easy-going, and love to fish, feast, dance and drink Kava drink.

The Indians may eventually buy them out, they are workers and savers.

It would be too bad, since these once so isolated people have resisted selling their lands to British, French and other once mighty colonial powers for so long. But, slowly, the islands are, one by one, being sold off. One to Malcolm Forbes. Raymond Burr to Buba Freejohn…now there is a genuine kook-ball if I ever heard of one.

The rest of the roster of cases in the court in Suva were Indians versus Fijian, and in every one–fisticuffs, slapping a neighbor's child, the judge remonstrating with everyone to forgive and forget, in short, to reconcile. So veddy public school British. Not bad advice, particularly on this level, though it did make him seem like a cross between Elmer Gantry and a Y.M.C.A. sports director.

The police in these courts were to die for. Sturdy, mostly handsome Polynesian, they were got up in the most bewitching and amusing garb I've ever seen–outside a Gilbert and Sullivan production, that is.

Mufti jackets with brass and epaulets, very military-looking. Peaking military hats. And with this–skirts, white or pastel, tapering to long points around the calf, just below the knee. How fetching, how Melrose Avenue, how Valentino!! The men, serious and comfortable, bottomed off these duds with flat, open sandals. Love those tropical mores and folkways–with a nod to costume designers and makers of the old braining clubs, which had spikes and hooks literally to open the skull to allow the brain to be removed more easily, to be of course, eaten. That ensures the winner will incorporate the courage, skill and wisdom of his enemy.

The police in Fiji look proud, happy and seemingly have one of the best jobs around in the land.

In counter-distinction to the U.S.A., where being a policeman is not a highly respected endeavor, unfortunately. Here they are called cops, fuzz, pigs.

In London, they bustle and have considerable clout, still. There they are called bobbies.

In France, they are "*le flic.*" Or gendarmes. And except in the colonies, like Tahiti, are not all that respected, it seems, although they take themselves very seriously. My sources for these opinions are two trips to Tahati, plus lots of French films, so attention, *zut alors* and *tout de suite.*

I don't know what the Aussies call their police; maybe I'll put in a call to the Australian travel agency and ask, but they seem to like them fine; rugged individuals they are too, one and all.

Didn't get to any Aussie courts this visit, because it was between Christmas and New Year's, and there were no proceedings in court at all.

In Canada, naturally, the mounted (on horseback) police are grand, and they, and we, love those red-jacketed Mounties–the shades of Nelson Eddie and Jeanette McDonald haunt their barracks and are resurrected at every glimpse.

In Texas, the American West Rangers fare better than most. Sheriff is a term form Arabia, where they were originally shariffs.

The old cop-hating attitudes seem to have gone with the 60s, except for the virulently hated South Africa cops who are slugging black women and children over the heads in the nightly televised mayhem from Africa.

Uniforms are splendid things, I think, and give their wearers a sense of clan, tribe, bonding and cohesiveness still revered and cherished beneath our modern exteriors. They speak to the primitive core of us...that's very much alive and well beneath our Calvin Kleins.

Uniforms give that pull of authority. With self-confidence, perseverance, and yes–good tailoring—a man can go anywhere in this world.

(Oh, I learned a wonderful thing today! I learned to convert celsius to farenheit. Multiply by 2, add 30. To reverse: subtract 30, divide by 2. And my family thinks I'm hopeless at math. Ha!)

OJ TRIAL

I think we have made a big mistake in giving up as a royal colony. Sorry for the revanchist views, but folks, all you have to do is to look at your TV every night. Even the all no-Jay stations sneak peeks into the trial every day, at least here in L.A. they do. Leno has a hilarious skit about the trial every night on his show. And I agree with him, that it is unfortunately, the comedy event of the century. I mean, with Dan Quayle, there was a blooper every six months or so, with Jerry Ford we had to make do with an occasional assaulted golf game bystander or a trip up the steps to an airplane every once in a while.

But with O.J., by God, it is the Gong Show each and every court day. There is some outlandish ploy on the part of the Desperate Defense to try to inject reasonable doubt that this oh so obviously guilty man did not do the deed.

The majority of people in this state, probably in the country, feel that their precious hero must have been framed. I don't care what the facts show, they think us establishment folk are out to get this black man who clawed his way up from the projects of San Francisco. Certainly this had been a realization of the great American Dream. Exactly like Elvis.

Both larger than life people, handsome, charismatic, one immensely talented in music, the other a brilliant athlete coming from the most profoundly dirt-poor levels of society. But O.J. is, on top of a darling public persona, a symbol to a much oppressed minority of one of their own making it. And dopey Michael Jackson, to whom I have been mentally giving the benefit of the doubt since his alleged victims have been teenagers and not young children or babies, has thrown in his support for this famous figure. As Jackson has unwisely said, the American people want to tear down all famous black people.

There is nothing at all similar in the legal problems of these two popular icons. Jackson's victims were delivered to him by their unwise parents, and furthermore had a mouth and could have complained, or told the police. Nicole and Ron Goldman had no such choices about their lives. Jackson murdered no one, Jackson beat up no one.

All evidence, his history and his profile of narcissism, rage and violence points to him as it. The peril.

However…he is, in a most primitive sense of the word, American royalty…ensconced in the psyche and soul of his fans, as deeply as the British people treasure their monarchs whether or not they misbehave, are icons... right or wrong. Sacred symbols of a deeply held loyalty, on the level of religious enthusiasm.

Just look at football fans. There are people who astonish me by being sane, appropriate and level-headed, except when their favorite team is in peril. Then these same folks go certifiably ballistic; the team means something more than a sports event, it touches some core issues. For those who identify with a particular team or entity, its losses or failures are the same as their own. Thus the endless outpouring of support for O.J.

0.J.'s book is a best-seller, he is making tons of money from signing cards and pictures, statues, every kind of memorabilia, and 88 per cent of black men in this country think that he is innocent, that he has been framed by the police. After all, it took Rodney King two trials to get any justice. Jurors have black fathers, brothers, boyfriends or husbands who have likely been hassled in some racist way.

In spite of well-documented beatings of Nicole, which are indicators of a vicious streak, jurors may think only of the charming sports figure and deny with all their hearts the monster behavior.

There is a need to elevate him to the untouchable level. He didn't do it, but if he did, it wasn't that bad. She was a commoner anyway, who really cares about her or Ron.

We need to adore him, we will spend untold millions on his defense, parading one after another dim-witted, confused witness to try to reverse the mountain of forensics against him.

Even though the defense presumably screened out the most psychotic of the folks who volunteered to defend O.J. and witness for him, they are stuck with the most confused, motley assortment of benighted contenders for fame and fortune since the *Twilight Zone.*

TODAY'S TIMES

When I open my *Times* each morning, I know that Art Buchwald will be nattering away about surreal issues of Washington, D.C. The girls in apartment 3G will be speculating about other people's lives. Jack Smith will be smooth and philosophical about whatever—a vacation home in Baja, the library fire or his own heart attack. Erma Bombeck will predictably fulminate about lost socks, peanut butter stains or wrinkles in linen; all the housewifely frustrations.

The funnies are often not funny. Rather they are dour and dreary, a sort of printed soap opera, slow-paced enough to take a trip to Fiji, with stopovers in New Guinea and Borneo, and never miss a significant beat of a happening. Or at least one that isn't recapped and reprised in the following Sunday's edition.

Which brings me to the astrology feature. I watch with horror as day after day we are exhorted to be venal to the max; is this any way to run a culture? We are begged, today for instance, "to get on the right side of bigwigs." Do you love servility and apple polishing? "Cultivate higher ups" is another yucky one.

"Defer to those in a position to help my career." For crying out loud, what kind of apple-polishing boot-licking lackeys are working back there? Have you ever heard such cloying stuff, for even a self-respecting fortune-cookie maker would hesitate at this goop. Is this a logical outcome of two hundred years of enlightened capitalism and freedom? Making a living "the old-fashioned way," by licking someone's boots?

Then there's this wisp of subtle wisdom in a forecast: "be especially careful in moving vehicles today." Listen bud, this is Los Angeles, if I didn't take particular care every single solitary day I'd be history. I think they have a giant basket of these things, and they just keep rotating them from columnist to columnist and newspaper to newspaper. Some master cliché writer must have the residuals on them.

Here's a good one: "put harmony with mate at home in top priority for this evening." Give me a break! In L.A. you give top priority to your mate or you find yourself served with divorce papers and sitting in a single's bar so fast your head, as well as your bar stool will spin. The divorce rate is so high around here some men have been known to be propositioned on their way out to lunch in case they have changed their minds about married life since breakfast. Notes have been put in pockets by women who have heard the little woman is to be at her computer class that night, and are willing to keep husbands "company" for the evening—just in case he should feel amorous or lonesome. If they know what's good for them, every mate should keep close track of his partner at all times, and check frequently for dissatisfaction factors.

Another outstanding piece of advice: "get your personal effects in order early in the day." If I could manage that, would I be wasting good time reading the drivel in the astrology column? If I were tidy Virgo or a logical Taurus, would I be wasting time reading this astrology advice? Of course not. I read until smitten by an idea to write, a fresh new idea, natch. Not that I really believe in sun signs, but only flaky narcissistic Leo would ever think she should write a personal column herself.

Oh heck, I only do it to see my name in print.

MEDIA MOMENTS AND MEANINGS… OR, THE KISS

I never thought I'd have to look to *L.A. Law* for guidance or lessons in living. After all, I am among the professionals people come to and pay for their guidance, although we all know therapists want to uncover *your* goals, not impose theirs on you, don't we. Well, don't we? I can barely believe, myself, that I had to learn the hard facts of life about both kissing, and voting, from that program, which I have to speed home from a senior case conference on Thursday nights in order not to miss. And I'm not even mentally retarded, like Bennie!

It seems ridiculous, all right. It's not like I am emerging from a monastery, or divorce, into the world of osculations and civic duties. No, not at all.

It so happens that they do not announce that you have to put the ballot into slide *before* you put the red pins through the holes. I have been stall-worthily trying to do my civic duty, every four years for a very long time without sliding the ballot in the container. It was not easy to that way…it was very very hard.

I often thought, no wonder so few people turn out, it's very confusing with all these different numbers to keep track of. Embarrassing…God only knows who I've really been voting for all these years. So I'm not mechanically inclined, I never claimed I was. But I carefully read the instructions at the top of the ticket, and nowhere did they say to slide it in. I just thought you laid it on top. We all know 67% of folks cannot make their vcr's work, and women of my age are generally functional innumerates like illiterate only with numbers instead of letters. I've had my car five years and am only now almost succeeding in setting the automatic radio settings. I'd sure love to just have one button for each setting instead of scanning each time I want to get KFAC or KREW.

The kids and Hubby marvel at my ineptness; I announce it's part of my charm and that I never claimed to be Albert Einstein. Secretly, I am thrilled I can drive a car and make my word processer (more or less) work, although I have yet to be able to mail a floppy with one item on it through the mail, as I had hoped. Two different 'puter tutors have given up on me; well actually we sort of gave up on each other. We just wore each other all out. I keep needing younger teachers and fresher faces. What can I tell you; I clearly wasn't there when they handed out the spatial relations and mechanical genes.

Anyway, when Arnie taught the mentally sub-par Bennie how to vote in *L.A. Law*, the light bulb went on, and I said to myself, aha, that's what's been wrong.

And that is a lot more understandable that the recent lesson I absorbed form Tom Cruise's girlfriend teaching Dustin Hoffman's autistic character in *Rain Man* how two people are supposed to be kissing, circa 1989. She did both the didactic, and the experiential part. Explaining that the trick to it was to pretend you were tasting a delicious piece of fruit…then she opened her mouth and proceeded to slurp him. (In an elevator, no less.)

That was it. The proof positive that it's been *me* who's been wrong for the last five years.

I have been scandalized by all the open-mouthed kissing that's been going on in movies and TV, and have not been able to relate to it all. I've believed only couples on their honeymoon (and in the final stages of foreplay); either that or "bad" girls, prostitutes or Saint Bernards enjoyed and practiced such amatory indiscretions. It *still* reminds me of two dogs, or polar bears, greeting each other…a lot of teeth there, bub.

In my day a kiss was a distinct entity, having its own enjoyments and entitlements. It could be counted on to be pleasant and entirely satisfactory for what it was. What it was *not* was wet, gooey, or anything involving bodily organs to be stuffed down any orifices. *That* was called love-making, and was generally reserved for occasions when two people knew one another slightly better.

It seems the kiss I knew and loved in Williamsport circa 1949 has gone the way of the copper penny, an anachronism in its own time. No one uses it anymore, except I think to kiss their dogs and cats. People are slurped. I have even had to restrain my very own husband from starting out too moistly when wishing to show affection, I say *starting*; certainly there is a place for the exchange of bodily fluids but I don't think it is in the first five seconds of an embrace. Or on top of the rose parade float, either. Did you see that young couple, married on New Years' Day at the Rose Parade? It's a wonder his tongue didn't freeze fast to her chin, it was so cold and he was being such a *canine* with her…apologies to the real bow-wows here.

It may be sexual revolution has hit its logical end.

AIDS is restoring monogamy; I heard on the six o'clock news last night that some researchers think it is quite possible, even likely that AIDS virus can be transmitted in the saliva, and be spread that way. Ha, wouldn't that be a vindication for Puritanism.

Meantime, I'm gratified to see that Michael Jackson (the BAD one, not the KABC one) and the comedians on the late-night comedy shows on ABC and HBO have quit touching their genitals. For a long time, this was positively a fetish of rebellion on the late night shows, and you could picture mommies and nannies everywhere madly squirming as the their now grown-up charges defiantly touched themselves "down there." Hitching, adjusting and holding: the ultimate no-nos in public. I love comedy, but I sure hated the exhibitionism. TV comedy shows have become a favorite thing of mine on TV—that way I don't have to watch all of Carson to get to the comedian. *And* I don't have to endure the late hour hassle of being out and about on the strip to watch new talent. Most of all, I don't have to breathe cigarette smoke which is endemic to those milieus.

Thus me and the media are co-adjusting to each other, willy or nilly. Though I never thought it would happen to a hip chick like me,. I guess I too am a product of my time and place. Perhaps the pendulum is creeping back a bit? Too early to say. Anyway, the real test will be when they conquer AIDS and find a really good contraceptive device, one that works and is unobtrusive. Till then, I may let the media be a guide as far as voting, but keep my tongue to itself, and let the worldly scoff if they must and taste all the other folks they want to. I have a mighty discriminating palate for food *and* people; I sort of like it that way.

THE BIG CITY

Sunday morning, I am purusing *The New York Times* magazine section, which I do second on Sundays. First, I catch up with the really serious business of the funnies in *The L.A. Times*. *The New York Times* magazine section is beloved by me for Russell Baker's column, *Sunday Observer*, my favorite column of all time. Next best, I like the William Safire column.

I muse on my weekend so far: Last night we joined the beautiful people for dinner at IL Giardino. Hubby is recently returned from a five-month trial in Bakersfield and not gotten his bearing yet in the huge and unfamiliar city that L.A. has become to him since he has been gone. This restaurant is one we have been wanting to try, but hadn't yet gone.

H. being a lefty, whenever we set off someplace, his gyroscope starts wildly spinning and then characteristically goes tilt—meaning he wants plans and assurances, something like the certainty of success of an Allied landing on the Normandy beach on D-Day the sixth of June. Because of the eccentric-functioning directional cells of his brain, not malfunctioning, no, sometimes he does not want to go right or correctly, but usually when there is a strong passion on his part to turn, say north, it is a dead certainty that we need to go south. He's that kind of fun guy, but not always—he fluctuates like a magnet around iron filings in a blizzard.

I am a more freewheeling type myself and trust to intuition, my kin esthetic senses and the fact that I pre-cruised this restaurant to get a feel of where it is in preparation to making a reservation for the evening. So we set off. We argue at every corner. We have mighty tugs of war at each intersection as we get closer. He insists on turning right on Burton Way. I become steely in my determination not to circle round and round and the snippy tone of voice in my statement that I am driving the car and know where I am going. We turn left. We get there!

The tension has been as intense as if we were about to overshoot our airspace into the enemy territory of Irkutsk, Siberia (I love the name of that town, it sounds so irked and annoyed).

Well, hearts slow down, the sweat dries on our foreheads—another safe anchorage at a dangerous Saturday night restaurant rendezvous. No space craft passengers sagely landing at Cape Kennedy feel more relieved to be back from the mighty vacuums of space than we do as we drive into valet parking at the restaurant.

Once inside, very early for L.A.—sevenish—I settle down and begin to enjoy the parade of the beautifully dressed. This season's clothes are a blessing to me—very long loose tops, flared, A-shaped or trumpet skirts and big shoulders. Absolutely perfect for virtually camouflaging a person's body.

Now mine needs camouflaging and I am grateful. I look fairly graceful in these duds but why do people who have good figures dress like this? I have to buy up lots of this style before the teensy, skinny, minimalist stuff predicted for springtime hits the fashionable this winter in our shoulder pads that give us the look we want. They are always slipping forward, flopping around. When I watch the *Johnny Carson Show* they do that, at luncheons they do that, at plays, at parties, every woman I know is nervously pushing her shoulder pads back out of her minestrone or bowl of borscht or dish of *pate de foie gras* depending on the formality of the occasion. We all act like a cross between Joan Crawford and Knute Rockne this holiday season of 1985. God, I hope figures never come back!

GREECE AND LONDON

The divine beauty of the Classical period sculptures! (My mother's brother and also their father, Robert, have classical Greek profiles—again the connection seemed so clear.) The Greeks, Egyptians, Persians, and many, many tribes to the South, North, East and West conquered or were conquered, mingled and shipped back and forth from Africa, Asia Minor, and Europe. Alexander's troops got all the way to the Danube, overcame legions of tribes and territories with names such as Ilyria... why not my grandfather's?

The most poetic breakfasts I ever consumed were Greek: divine yoghurt with bowls of new honey and pomegranate particles; even grapes in giant bowls. Vines and trees loaded down in late September with ripe pomegranates and green grapes.

GREECE

The Athens airport. Have been told it is the pits. We had plenty of opportunity to do research there—we spent vast amounts of time there coming and going, and commuting to other islands.

My first surprise was, though one always thinks of Greece as Europe—have another think! There is a Northern European continent that comes and goes from this airport—but the Third World contingent vastly overwhelms.

Besides British Airways and Lufthansa, these airways fly out to Athens:

Alitalia
Egypt Air
El Al
Syrian-Arab Air net
Balkan-Bulgarian Airlines
Saudi Arabian

… and of course good old Olympic Airlines, the one we used to get to Rhodes and Crete, and from Rome to Athens.

Some of the passengers were in Borgues and Burberry's...some in Burnoose, Caftain, head-gear of every conceivable description, fabric, and wrap—and faces. Magnificent portraits right out of the Old Testament. Many people sprawl, asleep; Anglo types generally sitting stoically upright. Folks from older and hotter climes using the time to sleep or at least, to recline. Folks like us—even with a seven hour delay while two British Airlines Tri-Stars broke down—still erect and holding up appearances. (Our delay was considered piddling. At 8:00 p.m., a huge wave of clapping started cresting at the north end of the terminal and rolled down toward the duty free shops. We looked up, puzzled, at the arrival-and-departure screen. The flashing green light indicated that New York passengers were now boarding. Seems they had been waiting for their plane since

Friday [which caused those of us bound for London since 2:30 pm., Sunday to subside meekly.)

From the glorious harbor at Rhodes we could actually see Turkey. Harbor flanked by walls, ancient sprawling fortifications intended, sometimes unsuccessfully, to repel the periodic hordes of invaders which descended at intervals from Venice, Turkey, Sicily and Bulgaria to try and occupy this strategic and bounteous fortress island. The fort is so picturesque, with vast courtyards, vaulted ceilings, intricate, ancient, and charming winding streets of the old city. Within the fortress walls shops bustle with trade as in the days of the Order of the Knight of St. John.

(Amazing how modern the idea of not waging war is—to most of the world's people till very recently, war was seemingly the greatest moral and ethical enterprise of an individual's or society's life. The most glorious buildings, statues and art pieces were dedicated to warriors for God, their tribe nation. Although ancient Greeks and Aztecs had games: ball, courtyard, and Olympic—these games were generally a prelude to—or celebration afterward—of war, or in Alexander's case, the Macedonian way of marking the funeral of a great man. War games, that is.)

The blue and white stripes of the Greek flag stand for—as I'm told—freedom or death. Our driver for the day on Crete told us many stories of the legendary bravery of the Cretans and other Greeks during World War II, including the resistance and partisan activities of his own father. Considering how poor most of the countrymen are, it is a wonder they have not yet succumbed to the communist and socialist pall to the North. Albania looms, gray and bleak and joyless, directly to the North. The only time I ever saw Harry Truman looking heroic is when I got a glimpse of his giant statue on Crete—a marker of the one who injected enough money after World War II to help save Greece from the downward slide into Communist depression and suppression.

LONDON PART ONE—SHOPPING

It's my third day in London and I've got my routine cozied down to an art. On Monday morning, after arriving in the middle of the night in Athens because of the British Airways breakdown; I did everything wrong, I think, from a sense of desolation at separating as my husband went off to work and left me for six daytime weeks on my own. I slept late, thereby frustrating the chambermaids, walked much too far to the shopping center, and sprained a knee. Did not look right at intersections and had cabs turning corners almost onto my toenails.

Came out of Harrods at 5:00 p.m along with 10,000 other shoppers to find a pouring sky and a huge stampede of people wanting a cab. A harried Harrods doorman stormed about threatening to quit because people were not staying in a neat queue. I surveyed the mob and walked home: laden and blistered. Sweating and crackling with VAT vouchers and receipts. (God forbid I should need to return anything.)

The next day, sprained but wiser, I had a pocketful of change I was puzzling over. When I got "God-bless-you-Madam's" and surprised "Thank you, Madam's" from doormen and cabbies, I realized my unconscious wish to equalize the dollar to the pound was not wise. It did not work out so well for me in glorious Greece, and I always came out much ahead that way.

However, this was stickier. Fair details, let alone bargains, were not going to happen at this rate (literally).

So, I am now telling myself to figure closer to two dollars per pound if I want to eliminate the astonishment of lottery winner from those I wish to thank, but not pension off, for life.

Now I shop, do errands, have a grapefruit juice and fresh Greek salad at the health food bar at Harrods, collect myself and packages into a taxi and get home by 2:30 p.m. No jabs or mobs. Get to my room and order tea for one—plenty of extra hot water and lemon slices.

LONDON PART TWO—THE GORING HOTEL

Every great up must have its down.

For three weeks—to the day—I have accommodated to every delay; every short sandy bed, some with ants, every miscalculation that had us traveling 18 hours a day. With the aid of multivitamins, frizzling emergency C with potassium and extra vitamin B, I have delighted and astounded myself at my new found heartiness. Heretofore I have been very prone to viruses, flu, colds and allergies. My psychoanalysis has had a distinct and palpable effect, more well-being physically as well as mentally.

But yesterday we were moved from very cozy digs at the Goring Hotel to the most recently decorated and distinguished suite 54. However smart its pastel greens and pinks and freshly appointed flowered chintzes, there is no working heat. So after a full day of strenuous shopping at Harrods and Selfridges, came back to the (boring) Goring to find the bellman had moved all our packed cases—and the lovely suite was chilly and dark as the Tower of London before a beheading. It didn't matter anyways that the guest would be catching her death from a chill; since the stuffed up nose, not to mention the headache, would shortly be an annoyance of the past.

So today I sit on my salmon settee chatting with Suzy about whether she would draw the nets—sheer curtains along with the nightshades or leave the daylight in. I vote to let in whatever gray sullen daylight that will come. It is drizzling ever so slightly. The room is a clang with rings of metal room heaters that the night porter has supplied to stave off misery. The last suite had room heaters in every area, including the separate, elevated potty-room heater. That was the best: an hour with the room heater on and the door closed dried all daily undies and washed nightgowns better than my drier at home. I'd soak them in the magic green foam bath, take them into the tiled bathtub to rinse, let them drip dry on the shower attachment while I bathed in the piney residue—and voila! The clothes and I would emerge in an hour very clean, dry and smelling strongly of piney woods.

LONDON PART THREE—LARGER FITTINGS

"Larger Fittings"–found a special shop where there is a feeling of ease and acceptance. You are a *person* who needs, well, proper fittings. Not an ignoble large size. Forever. Immutable. Ordained. Fated. Prophesized. Preordained. Just a well, lovely attractive person needing some tactful and delicate attentions (at the moment.)

I enjoy the implication of the flux, of change, in this designation. After all, the wording is *larger fittings*. What goes up, must come down. After larger fittings (and a long bleak winter), might not smaller fittings follow? Possibly accessorized by shoes in narrow (rather than Ladies' Wider Fittings for shoes)?

Before I came to England, a friend convinced me to soothe my pet phobias about:

A) Not being warm enough;

B) Having nothing to wear;

C) Not finding a thing in my size.

… in case of the above contingencies, to stock up at the Forgotten Woman on Wilshire.

Somehow I feel flattered and accepted by this British designation of larger fittings. It makes me feel, "well, of course we can fit you dearie—why ever not?" Like, well, right now you need a 22. A fitting is an active word implying change, ebb, and flow. Though, to be absolutely honest, there's been more flowing than ebbing in my eating scheme. *Large sizes* imply this is it. you're stuck, toots. You'll always be porkers.

"Larger Fittings" seems to delicately suggest you're having a bad day. Ordinarily, of course, you'd be at your accustomed rack at Yves St. Laurent or Valentino.

Oh no. No longer for me the faintly sad and plaintive Forgotten Woman of Wilshire and Bedford. She feels *too* sorry for herself. She's not forgotten, nor is she to be chided or made to feel conspicuous or guilty about an extra pound or two...

... but just today—actually, all week—has been impossible, my dear. Adjustments have to be made for well, previous indiscretions. One manages.

Implicit in larger fittings is...Smaller Fittings. Just around the corner, of course, all these things we can just take in again.

Fittings, you see.

A plural verb, not a singular static condition, but one that contains the promise of adjustments, seams, tucks, gussets, smocking.

An altogether different tone is set in some American and a type of brazen British shops, which I can thoroughly eschew.

LONDON PART FOUR—MUSINGS

In London: at first newspapers and TV seemed so uninteresting—issues and people nobody cared about.

But slowly became extremely interested in the byplay between Arthur Scargill of the Mineworker's Union and Ian McGregor, of the National Coal Board. Got used to a debased BBC, now showing British versions of stupid American sitcoms, instead of their previously superb programs. Even the erstwhile and elegant London Times has been sold and sordid-ized. But one adjusts.

Now back in L.A.—am not interested in our news—not yet. We are space travellers in orbit still, neither here nor there.

Came back on Nov. 3rd in time for a gigantic overdose of political treacle. One-half hour of gazing at TV's version of the election process makes my head ache. I do not intend to vote for the top of the ticket. I really like Reagan, but cannot emotionally vote for him. My head won't let me. Much more important, my kids would probably boycott me forever. In the primaries, in our family, #1 son voted for Jesse Jackson, #2 wrote in a vote for Barry Commoner. Hubby tossed in with Mondale, and I threw in with Gary Hart. I go for a good hair and environmental issues every time.

I like feeling prosperous, strong and non-guilty, that's why I like Reagan.

I am going to follow Dane's advice on all the issues, however. I agree with him on everything local. He also is an environmental science major at UCLA.

Quite a coincidence—on the plane coming home a film with Goldie Hawn, who I said to my seatmates was becoming the new Sally Field, playing a gutsy young American who goes to work in an airplane plant when her husband enlists after Pearl Harbor.

(That airplane plant, by the way, is really the Hughes Plant opposite the Lopez Ranch stand on Jefferson Blvd. in Culver City, on your way to the Marina.)

I could so identify with the values and mores of that era, as I was almost her age at the time. I too was a product of women in the home minding the family of the Post-War forties and fifties which sure helped to put me where I am today, and that is struggling to find my identity and complete my education. Okay, so I'm slow. Okay. Watched while the bee did a little dance around and around the page. I moved slowly away as the dance heated up. Finally after five minutes or so, the bee proceeded to a jig or perhaps it was flamenco. He stomped around some more, and then flew off. Before I could intone the "Goodbye my brother" which I had planned for the occasion—he flew on my bare shoulder and bit the living shit out of me. I ran to the rented car and sat in it, away from treacherous, ungrateful vermin until my husband returned much later, unbitten, laden with the spoils of a very successful shell hunt.

At that, I ceased and forbore:

apologizing to flowers before I picked them;

thanking radishes and lettuces before I cut them for salad;

thanking the powers that be in meditation for protecting me from the pain of the world's assault. From now on, I trust nothing, yell loudly and brandish a big can of Raid.

LONDON PART FIVE—CHECKS AND STRIPES

I could buy all of London and sometimes feel I'm doing it, a little at a time, with all the luscious wool, cashmere, and leather that fits me here. Also found great bookstores with publications I've not been able to find at home. A very decent, fair price for the exceptional quality of the books. Further things I've learned:

Hubby must have some British genes. In L.A., I frequently blast him as we are about to go out together for the evening about dressing in a checked suit, a different checked shirt, a polka-dotted tie and another disparate type of handkerchief or cap. I remonstrate, I nag. Sometimes, he changes; I beam. Sometimes he won't; I sulk.

Here in London, I am truly a-boggle, not to say a-goggle, at the outfits seen on Brits high and low alike. The average walking or bus-riding chap on the street generally has two to four different checks on; one type on his cap, one on his scarf, one on his jacket—and there could be trousers, hankies, clan ties, etc. to further confound one.

The upper classes are the same, only about stripes. With my own eyes I have witnessed heads of large companies and leaders of Ministry level wearing striped suits, gray on black; striped shirts. Usually white with gray stripes, or gray with darker stripes—and striped ties—sometimes muted, with the stripes woven in. *And* if you please, one had a polka-dotted tie in navy and emerald dots big as cat's eyes. Wow. In L.A., businessmen are much lower-keyed, solid, and muted. That is – if they're not in high-status blue jeans or tennis togs—*de rigueur* for entertainment lawyers making upwards of 250 thousand a year. Dollars, not pounds.

You know what? It's easy to do—wear a whole lot of plaids. I had a shopping frenzy at the Scotch Shop yesterday for two reasons. Number one, it took too many buses to get to the zoo. Number two, my chest hurts outdoors. So I hopped on my beloved 52 from Victoria and got out at the Scotch Shop. There I bought tartans galore—so, Hubby wore out to dinner his new Burberry tie, it's Harrods brown and beige check cashmere cap. In one short shopping spree, I had made him into the quintessential Brit. I forgot the very subtle brown plaid shirt. But the Aquascutum raincoat was solid navy. Our host of the weekend got himself up snappily in beige trousers, blue and white checked shirt, blue and brown checked tie, brown and white checked jacket. You see?

I am now not *above* wearing my red Lesli border plaid skirt with my new Royal Stuart scarf and cap.

But those elegant, tall, stunning upper-class men with stripe on stripe! Might there not be subliminal fixation left over from World War II—stripes equaling promotion? As in earning your stripes? Might it not be residual empire archetype—tropics, jungle, zebra?

I can understand the Scots—clan/tribal love for plaids. The stripe fetish and gangster could dare such outfits. Maybe being so close to zero longitude has collectively gone to their heads.

TRAVELLING NORTH

I didn't used to be so phobic when I was younger. Does this sentence structure frazzle your nerve endings? Sorry, I'm from Pennsylvania Dutch country. In younger days, at the prospects of a trip; I would throw a toothbrush and warm skivvies in the old knapsack, and bright-eyed and bushy-tailed, off I would go. Buy me a ticket, and meet me at the airport in thirty minutes, I'd be there.

No more. Having a general tendency to need more and more stuff when I travel, last year kind of finished off a certain *joie de vivre* I fear might be gone for good. We sallied forth to Fiji for Christmas, only to encounter a world-class cyclone while visiting tiny Douglas Island, an hour by plane from the main island of Vitu Levu. This blow up had me quaking in my coconut-thatched hut for eight days, the result of, as we now know, the greenhouse effect on the earth, that will see larger and larger hurricane systems spawned as the result of all the nefarious gas ratio imbalances around nowadays.

I've been wary of exotic climes since we survived that fiasco, and thought we'd take a tame, though gorgeous vacation trip up the coast and re-visit beautiful Cambria, Monterey, Carmel and Tomales Bay for the ten days before Labor Day.

Because I could stuff the back seat, packing was a piece of cake; it was *un*packing that now makes me nervous. There is more of me, subsequently more fabric to cover the more of me than in the old days. And I've accumulated more stuff. Although hotels try, God knows they try to ease the burdens of the traveler by supplying what all people need; soap, shampoo, sometimes bathrobes and paper slippers, they have not begun to be able to deal with my requirements. I still need my portable:

Water pik
Electric anti-plaque toothbrush, inter-plaque
Eye drops for dry eyes
Toe Lotion (against athlete's foot)

Baby powder

Sunscreen (this should be given everywhere)

Back issues of *International Journal of Psychoanalysis* in case I'm feeling guilty about not keeping up in the field.

The latest S.J. Perlman compilation of letters to read in case the journal articles get me down.

Enough dental floss, mouth wash, and Sensodyne tooth paste to ward off the endodontist till September.

Decongestants, anti-histamines and nose spray to keep the pollens at bay.

My own pillow...who can sleep on a strange pillow in the middle of the night?

In short, I *don't* leave home without it, whatever *it* might be.

More and more paraphernalia is miniaturized; they're making it, I'm buying it. So why doesn't it all get easier? Because it all has to work, that's why. And because you have to remember where you packed it. And find it. And *do* it.

A word on those hotel kimono bathrobes, built as one size fits all. In my experience, one size fits no one, absolutely no one at all. Hubby's kimono belt is tied under his armpits, giving scant protection to the top of his thighs, making him resemble nothing so much as an x-rated Jack Lemmon in *Some Like it Hot.*

That same size does not go the distance, decency-wise on me. Either I'm okay in the legs, or it's circumference-wise I'm in trouble. Besides the belt around the waist, I also have to clutch the screaming terry cloth above and below the waist to avoid just blowing the wind. As it is, a full third of me, and the prime cut, I may add, is precariously close to the big chill. The robe is hanging on by a thread, I am quietly vowing to get myself to Nutri-system, it's a mess. I think they make these damned things in Hong Kong for folks 1/3 of our size, to sabotage our self-confidence so they can pick up more gold medals at the next Olympic Games. Hey, it's paranoia and it's mine.

Spontaneity certainly has lessened as far as snap decisions go to take up interesting travel invitations. All right and conform to doctor's orders. I have to worry about looking respectable *and* still be able to sight-see, which means a clever choice of shoes. I don't want to wear my all-purpose Nike Airs, and the orthopedic loafers make me feel like Grandma Moses. Ah, the joys of SAS, they have spring, are leather and can be found at Nordstrom's in every size and width. I get to feel comfy and look fairly passably dressed up.

I must tote along extra calcium against bone loss, estrogen to replace what I'm losing, and all my armamentarium to continue fighting in the holy wars against plaque and cholesterol. Ye gods, the crisps, the fibers, the popcorn that must be bagged up and bundled along. Modesty precludes enumerating those items that service more personal venues, (as we say in the Olympics); suffice it to say, the pharmaceutical companies and Madison Avenue are busy cashing in on guilt and phobias they produce. They want us to purchase products for areas only pointed to on ivory figurines by formerly well-bred Chinese ladies.

AUTUMN IN LOS ANGELES

What a blow, what a shock—the street near my home that I depend on to revive the precious experience of autumn for me, Loring, west of Hilgard off Sunset, has certainly let me down. The City Officials, in their infinite wisdom, have shorn the maples of their glorious limbs, all the way down to punk, to army G.I. cuts, instead of the long lush gorgeously flowing limbs and leaves of a month ago. What a heartless, stupid mutilation for a leaf-freak like me. Just as bad as pruning the rose bush just as the buds are popping open. Now at long last, just when the leaves are at their most magnificent vibrant peak of color—for L.A.—at long last the weather is ideal for crisp walks under gold and scarlet deciduous gloriousness. Starting in September, I used to look so eagerly forward to the fall leaves. I always wanted to go for a ride to the mountains, Arrowhead or Big Bear, to see the seasons change. That is because I am a Pennsylvania girl, born and bred. I have now learned that it is all quite different here in Southern California. One has to wait until late October or early November, this year actually late November, to really see significant stands of liquid amber, Japanese maple and real maple trees turning in the southland. Before then, the weather is so intractably, unrelentingly hot and smoggy—right through to November sometimes. A walk in even the moist woods is asking for heat stroke. At those temperatures, what I had better do are breast strokes in the swimming pool. So even the most wonderful back east kind of streets become mean streets to me.

But there is this brief, all too brief week or less when the leaves have turned and not yet fallen leaving their bare twigs, just such a day is November 22, 1985. (This day has heavy associations for me. My sister's birthday, John F. Kennedy's assassination—both disasters of a general or of a particular nature)—anyway, Loring is a grave disappointment today.

We've done a bit of travelling in our time and I lived in D.C. as a child when people plumb keeled over watching Fourth of July parades—it was a hardship post. But it had seasons. The summer cooled off, the winter thawed out. Some places we've visited had a range of temperature from awful hot to terribly hot to too god-damn hot altogether. For instance, four years ago in February, we landed at Denpasar, Bali. The waiting room was unbearably hot, but customs took only minutes. We stepped outside to the curb to get a cab, and then realized that the waiting room had been air-conditioned! The temperature was a cozy 120 degrees Fahrenheit. We finally had the most exotic vacation destination of them all—Hell!

As a matter of fact, the Balinese art, dance, leather and wood puppetry and mythology have very much to do with devils; the fight against them and their malignant influence seems to preoccupy these people. There are little shrines everywhere, public and private, and the most common artifact in Bali? The black-and-white checked sarong-type garment worn and pictured everywhere. I wondered why these dudes were all dolled up in Italian tablecloths! But I shortly found out the black and white symbolized the eternal, everlasting conflict between good and evil. Many seminal rituals of the Balinese have to do with outwitting evil beings or devil spirits—the shadow puppets dialogue with evil.

We witnessed a passage of rite for an adolescent boy and girl in our neighborhood temple one morning. Amidst plenty of cooking and food preparation, a boy and girl were carried around by their relatives atop gold colored thrones in full traditional headdress with many cantilevered turned-up corners—just what you would expect on the back lot of Twentieth Century Fox. Coming from Los Angeles, it is always something of a shock to realize things are real, not made of Styrofoam or part of a set! Then the youngsters had done to them what our guide assured us was "getting their tits filled." My Hubby and I blinked at this one and asked for many clarifications whereupon the guide vigorously said "tits filled." My brain reeled and my chest hurt in sympathy but we somewhat timidly awaited whatever was to happen although the only time I could imagine tits getting filled was when new born baby and mommy are reunited in the maternity ward!

Well the *teeth* are *filed* to a point, certain of them—the eye-teeth I believe, to ward off evil and to give the new man or woman a weapon with which to defend himself or herself. Sounds like a vampire culture, no?

Oh yes, anyway, back to West Los Angeles. So, bitterly turning my back on the emasculated, of the now boring Loring, I set out for other pockets of autumnal nostalgia and found some small but choice sites. One off Hilgard opposite UCLA to the east. Warner Street from Hilgard all the way to Wilshire—lovely! Next, a terrific pocket park behind the new post office south of Wilshire bordered by Veteran and Sepulveda—really swell and quite characteristic of Los Angeles for fall leaves were blazing cheek by blossom, as it were, with South American silk floss trees caparisoned with giddy pink orchidaceous flowers. Quite spectacular! A northern environment juxtaposed against this blush of springtime at its most dazzling culmination.

I like Montana Street from Ocean Avenue inland. Also, the street one block south is ablaze today. Random streets are planted with liquid amber in the attractive neighborhoods.

Between Montana and San Vicente Boulevard—the one with the coral trees, not the other commercial one.

Then a really big and beautiful surprise was Lincoln Boulevard from Santa Monica for a few commercial blocks oddly, briefly beautiful with crimson leafed trees.

Another lovely vista is Westwood Boulevard for four or five blocks south of Pico. Looks fuller and more foresty than any of the others this year.

Originally I forsook my usual October fantasies of going back to Pennsylvania or at least to Vancouver, we've seen several great autumns on trips there, for a central California trip. The Travel section of the *L.A. Times* assured me that if I set out to drive the spine of the Rocky Mountains, I would see plenty of turning foliage and since I was to be in and around Bakersfield on several October and November weekends, half-way to Lone Pine anyway, that would really work out. Well, it did not! What the article forgot to say was the time change. The dreaded, cursed, rotten "spring forward, fall back" time change. It makes me as depressed as a Scandinavian film maker. It makes me morose as a moose in the Caribbean. So, the time between travel time and winter pall, fall, gloom, doom and turning leaves left too little time to be worth it. You have to get where you are going and then stay put and go places on foot. This is one woman's guide to changing seasons right here at home.

Oh yes, another goody, Carmelina Drive east of Beverly looks wonderfully rustly and rustic, it really does.

The most notable shortcoming of even the most colorful streets in our part of the world is there is never a nice big build-up of scuffly, rattly, wonderful smelling leaves. The streets are clean with a leaf or three on the ground. There are squads, platoons, battalions of gardeners beating me to every pile of leaves everyday (particularly in Holmby and Beverly Hills); nothing gets a chance to accumulate and mingle. The streets smell clean and neutral. I remember, as Proust remembers his madeleine cookie and tea, the pungent earthy leaf smells of a dark wintry Williamsport, Pa. Halloween night when I was about ten years old scuttling along the black streets, really cold and very spooked, to join a couple of friends to trick-or-treat. I can see it and feel it right now and all my impressions and attitudes get resurrected along with this olfactory memory. I read somewhere that there is about to be visited onto our society something called scent therapy. Apple makes you calmer; Peppermint makes you hungrier; other scents make you other things. The point is good and true methinks; smells activate a much more primitive level of the brain and mind, more emotional and interesting, than mere words.

I am happy about Halloween and Thanksgiving because by then I have completed my mourning over the loss of summer, the beach, swimming in the pool, and the fun of going to Catalina to snorkel with outrageously flopping Garibaldi fish-like large orange goldfish. They are unique to this island. I also love to swim in and around the kelp at Catalina that grows to 40 feet and more in the ice cold saline off-shore forest. And no more trips to Laguna Beach to try its treacherous coastal tides outside the Sand-and-Sea Hotel. The water is rougher there than anywhere; I go in swimming (such an idyllic spot), how can one not venture in after all even if you do get roughed around a lot by the waves? I have been skinned there on rocks more than any place, even Malibu. Tried Santa Barbara this summer in July, but maybe Santa Barbara is good for autumn leaves; the water was then certainly too cold to swim there.

Oh god, it is fun to plan how to spend money although I never thought I was the materialistic type. I love to go places. I just read a cute gag in the rag that I treat myself to at the check-out counter of my neighborhood store; well, I am entitled to some reward for all that marketing! Plus, I am the only person in L.A. who admits buying *The Star*, *The Enquirer*, *The Globe*, etc., and I can't be the only one they publish for, now can I? Oh yes, the gag is or the squib is:

"Success for a man is measured by his ability to earn more money than his wife spends. Success for a woman, of course, is finding that man." Well, to offset this frank disclosure I will tell you, and you may or may not believe me, but I think I am the only person in Los Angeles who has not purchased even one teeny-tiny lottery ticket! Oh yes, by Halloween and Thanksgiving I had finally given up on my fantasies of (1) covering my swimming pool in order to swim through the winter, (2) buying a wet suit in order to do that same thing, (3) swimming in an ice cold pool with a friend to burn up billions of calories, and to keep from developing hypothermia, (4) decided it's finally great walking weather and if I can ever get my "stuff" together I am going to walk everywhere to thicken my bones and prevent osteoporosis and burn up calories and avoid pneumonia and *wait for summer again.*

Many strange people who emigrate to Los Angeles think it is always warm here. Well, of course, compared to what? Tahiti? No. Siberia? Yes. Key West? No. New York City in the winter? Yes. Virgin Islands? No. And so on. I wear wool, cashmere, boots and scarves in winter here. And spring is the worst, that is when it is cold and foggy as an old Sherlock Holmes movie; which is why, as much as I yearn to move to Zuma, Trancas, or Broadbeach in July, I don't really want to be there in March (my throat hurts just thinking about it). So now I am resigned to dressing warm and enjoying different spots. Exploring places that are too hot to visit in the summer inland places; the zoo, the arboretum, Descanso Gardens. However, I do creak on land. In the water I am seal-like, fluid and flabby, blubbered and buoyant. I couldn't sink if I wanted to. On land I have joint-aches, knee sprains, backaches; I may be part mermaid but must remember to wear bright colors and not tempt sharks when we get to the South Pacific next month. They might not notice I don't have whiskers and eat fish as I swim. Pear-shaped persons cannot be too careful.

This is the first I've written since a well-meaning friend advised me very earnestly to write everyday maybe two or three times a day. He scared me into rebellion, I refused to write a word and felt creatively constipated for a week afterwards. What a relief, to flow again. I've got a bushel full of homework to do and papers to write for school; I am also terrified I may not be allowed to keep up with my class cause I've been away so much. Equally terrified I will be allowed to keep up with my class and won't be able to do all the work-and so it goes. If it ain't one thing it's twenty others, as the poet says.

LONDON PART SIX—HOME AGAIN

Some thoughts while winging home to Los Angeles: the City of London—so beautiful architecturally—bridges, towers, medieval gates—mixed in mid-April mélange of woolens, cashmere, leathers, flowers, *flowers*! Runners-racing past London Bridge—bobbies, horse guards in gold spikes with vermilion capes all in a soup of fog, light rain, and fragrance of a million gold, white, lemon, short and long-trumpeted daffodils. Wandered through Hyde Park in the hour between reports of the London Marathon on BBC One. 9:30 A.M., April 17th, all senses dazzled by the sights, sounds, smells, textures, cool, fresh wet air intermixed with billions of tiny transparent flying mayflies. Huge round beds of flowers in Hyde Park—planted with tall-tall tulips striped with yellow-and-crimson blooming above multi-hued primroses. Purple swirls of short, fluffy petaled-tulips interspaced with purple primroses. Pink fat short tulips with matching prism. Burberries, Scots kilts—Harrods—millions of items of silver, flower, vegetable, silk, cheese, grouse, crayfish, oyster, a giant hodge podge of gorgeousness to eat or wear, drink or smell, gaze at or lie upon.

Near the Serpentine, two tiny bunnies, each about one month old, were nibbling on grass under a bushy edge, totally relaxed and skittish in the balmy fog. Brave British bunnies! Black and beige, glossy, with tiny pink-lined ears. Undaunted by gold-spiked crimson-caped horse guards thundering by. The Queen's rabbits? Serene against poachers?

Butterscotch geese blending to brown on the shore. Blackbirds with white badges on brows all wearing bands on legs.

Indian Restaurants interspersed with Barclay Bank offices on every other block. Sheiks and flunkies gravely parading around the lobbies of plush hotels (left over from the last OPEC meeting?). An entire bank of circular beds of lilies of the valley recognizable by the leaves of the thousand plants, breaking the ground, one or two showing forth a bell, sweet scented and exquisite; but we were there a week too soon.

8:00 a.m., London time, 1:00 p.m. Los Angeles time.

From the back seat in the first class, I see the ocean beading up with bits, then chunks, then shoals, then larger and larger pieces; finally, whole continent-sized ice snow covers with fiords of ocean between. First time ever seen—usually it is clouded over or night—obscured. The top of the world is so close I strain my eyes for long snow-blinded moments to see a polar bear or a pod of whales.

A sail up the Thames is like a trip backwards in time as features of old London loom up. A stroll up Bond Street is a preview of Paris couture. Vast riches in the National Gallery; Ingres supple and fleshy inundated with religious rococo. Drunk with color shape and smell at Kew Gardens. Vast planes of the most artful naturalness. Found a grove of cherry trees in full bloom; practically had a Nirvana experience of the highest joy, I was stretched out under one tree as faintly pink petals floated like a blissful blizzard to the ground around me. Enjoying the trees breaking into leaf; light-green, tightly curled leaf buds, fruit blossoms, just teasingly letting the tiniest rim of color betray variety, identification of species.

Giant ice flow beneath the plane. My compliments to the survival skills of polar bears. How can any mammal make a living on frozen water?

Two bad British plays; seven splendid British meals; horrible pub food; Jaguar and Rolls Royce trips. A week that ranged from twenty degrees Fahrenheit to seventy degrees Fahrenheit—that felt winter literally turn into spring from one day to another. Watching the BBC in London; reading reviews of Graham Greene in his own country; *The London Times* front-page stories –cheek by jowl with photos of baby Prince William, features about the cruelty of mouse racing and the need to exterminate this year's crop of gray squirrels before they exterminate the firs and spruces in the Commons. One up-close look at the Queen's horse being lovingly, glossily, magnificently led into the Queen's stable. More coverage on Princess Diana's smiles and outfits than those of Jackie O. in her heyday. Dover Sole Colbert at Wheelers—Bravo! Clotted cream on fruit cobbler! Lilting Britishisms: "Oh, Pardon!" for excuse me; "Sorry" for say again. The British use of weather—"we are having a bit of a *weather* over Scotland," meaning bad—good is never weather. And how extremely well they dress in neat, dark blue, and pinstripes, shod and pressed, gloved and hatted, immaculately. No matter how hard I try, I'm always linty, fuzzy and either too sparkly or too American; blue jeans and sweat suits glare American amidst bowlers and bankers.

In England, just a pearl necklace and earrings seem right and enough. One wants to be proper while strolling about Knightsbridge, not flashy.

Usually, something wildly barmy or fascinating on the tube; a diatribe about saving some kestrel hen or a program of arcane Indian religious music. Inscrutable cricket and soccer matches, a demonstration master bridge game, everyone sounding like a Monty Python send-up. (In fact, most people sounding straight out of *The Meaning of Life*, today.)

My very first trip – first class! The first three and a half hours of the flight being served pre-dinner drinks and crudités and so on until bursting. Service is amazing—I need nothing more now, thank you. But where, oh where will you be tomorrow when I need (would love, that is) some of this over-abundant service or at least a little pressure to accept food or drink. Scots – plaid clad stewardess, perky and beautifully spoken on British Caledonian airline. Fluffy and expensive red or blue plaid blankets over us. A total change of environment, freshened perceptions, avid interest in building, shapes, air quality, lifestyles, realization of how much normally we screen out, split-off, gray out in one's own home town.

Ice floes giving way to dreary gray land mass puddles with whitened water—Greenland? Iceland? No land at all or snow and water. Where can people start habituating? What marks human survival levels? Oh, I'll know when I see green growth below zero, nope, it's roads going from nowhere to nowhere that I can yet see. My map says we are either over Froebesher Bar or over Hudson Bay.

Down below—where do all the roads lead from, lead to? Nowhere to nowhere? Low gently sculptured land, black looking sticks of bare–boned trees, grayish black land receding to grayish—brown then brownish—gray, then clearly land as we know it in squares, now roads, a town, tiny but recognizable. The tundra ends, clouds begin—darn it! Just wondering if I was seeing Alaska for the first time or just Newfoundland again. Don't ever trust me on geography or math; I could be tens, hundreds or thousands off on either.

JOURNALS, BOOKS AND MUSINGS

Come to think of it, this journal is being written for my analyst. I didn't bring one of his books or articles with me as I usually do to feel close, so writing now seems the more direct contact. I will transcribe or tape this journal so he can share it when I return to L.A. In the meantime, the emotional and physical chore of writing does the trick form an enhancing feeling of well-being and contact closeness spiritually with him. As well as producing, know what? Just producing.

I have a fascinating book to read: Mary Renault's *Funeral Games*, the last of the Alexander trilogy. How she reconstructs a life and times from incredibly old sources before the Ptolemy's were Pharaohs of Egypt. Ptolemy was Alexander's right hand man, a Macedonian like Alexander.

Musing about my heretofore totally unconscious connections with Greece. There was a classical Philip in the last generation—my father's youngest brother. There is an Alexander in the next—my younger son. Another odd item is my gold jewelry. All the things I've acquired have been of classical Greek motif—a Gordian knot ring.. Alexander is said to have solved the riddle of the Gordian knot by simply slashing it with his sword. My other rings are a lion's head and tail ring, the tail encircling the finger. A Byzantine square with hand-hammered design stuck with a few sprinkles of gems. My earrings, an exact replica of ones I saw in the Anthropological Museum in Athens, worn during Alexander's time. Finally, my fascination with the palmette design which was seen adorning buildings, ceilings, roofs, statues at the Parthenon, and the bits and pieces which thankfully reside now in other places. Thankfully…because the smog plus the thundering feet of the visiting multitudes in Athens is crumbling all the original, glorious stone-and marble-work.

LONDON PART SEVEN—THINGS

Rhodes was the island for umbrellas and furs. Every third store would be an umbrella emporium where you could buy an umbrella and matching tote bag for 600 drachmas. Six bucks, American. I never bought one because younger son Dana Alexander had just given me a gaudy green and yellow one for my birthday in August. Fur stores and leather shops abounded. Didn't bother with either of those, because I hope my size will change for the smaller and they're too hard to alter.

In Crete—boots, boots, boots and ceramics, of which we bought a bunch of vases and plates, just gorgeous ware. In Athens, hand-hammered crafted gold jewelry. I got a lovely Greek key design necklace.

In London, wools and cashmeres and wonderful lined raincoats. One of each, plus fabulous socks, slacks, scarves and gloves.

Harrods deserves its own category. Eventually discovered the 52 bus and life has not been the same. Harrods 12-foot recently-dead shark draped over a seven-foot clamshell in the food hall. For sale, and all looking delectable; white-bait, prawns, sole, flounder, lobster.

Meats gloriously appealing. Fowl: small blackish looking grouse, partridge, a tiny bird, pale teal. Probably had feathers from which we take our color. Of course chickens, geese, ducks.

Whole aisles of pies: pork, grouse, vegetable, Cornish pies handmade in Cornwall, meat and vegetable pies of every description, all guarded round with pastry shells that looked to be 3/4 of an inch thick.

Glorious apples, 30 different varieties. I tasted the Kentish apple that was more savory than anything I've ever eaten—fragrant and crisp as supermarket apples rarely are at San Vicente Foods.

I long to get out to the country, from whence these luscious fruits come. Last Sunday took the boat trip from the embankment near Cleopatra's needle and powerful crouching Sphinxes, to

Greenwich. Even the rain did not spoil the delightful design of the painted chapel, with Athenian Wedgewood decor (painted moldings of classical Greek key, palmette and rosette executed in the richest of creamy beige, cocoa, teals and corals…) Past the colonnade, up the path through typical spacious English gardens with large stately trees in full leaf with yellow and golden hedges this October 7th...to the observatory of the royal astronomers and the Greenwich clocks quadrants and other scientific paraphernalia to make time exact. Zero longitude at last! (Wonder where zero latitude is? Probably in Ecuador. Equator? Exact middle of the earth?)

I will say it seems worth joining the Royal Navy to walk on these grounds and eat in the historic and splendid dining room replete with hundreds of handsome silver candelabra on the long oak tables surrounded by portraits and busts of Britain's finest. And visited once a year by the Royal Mum, who has taken a particular interest in the Naval Academy.

From the rosy apricot settee have moved to the bed and covers—what to do about all our weekend invitations? Ha—I'm kidding myself—it's bed for me. Hubby can go alone.

I have so much more time in England. I am not enticed by any of the wacky TV shows on coastal wave action or armadillos.

So I can read and write with more leisure.

LONDON PART EIGHT—FIVE WEEKS AT THE GORING HOTEL

Bumped into Mr. Goring himself in the lobby this morning—gray pinstriped cutaway and all. Since the N.C.B. pays our tariff every week, he knows who we are. Mr. G: "Out sightseeing this morning, are we?"

Me: "No, I'm trying to find the Karnack Book Shop in Gloucester Road today."

Mr. G.: "Oh, so far to go for books?"

Me: "Specialty store for psychoanalytic books." Mr. G." "Oh, if you're one of <u>those</u> people, I'm afraid of you."

Me: "No no, I'm perfectly innocent."

Laughter, fade.

Completed my errand, bought six hardcover books when I went in for a paperback, couldn't bear not to finish Herbert Rosenfield's *Psychotic States.*

Yesterday, cleverly took the 25 from Victoria Station to Selfridges, then made my way on foot up past Barrett St., home of traditional British, medicine. Thrilled to death and scared to turn in to 63 New Cavendish, home of London Psychoanalytic, felt like an imposter (didn't know enough to be studying there).Was politely greeted by the librarian, Jill Duncan, who asked what I wished to see. She quickly produced the asked-for Francis Tustin and Herbert Rosenfeld. I settled into a vast ancient green velvet armchair in the library—amazingly comfortable—but was instantly assailed by an anti-analytic intestinal insurrection. My avid perusal of Rosenfeld was interrupted by frequent trips to the mercifully nearby ladies'—but I <u>was</u> mortified by the undistinguished rumblings coming in the twilit silence of the venerable reading room—by my stomach lulled into a false state of relaxation by the reclining slope of the emerald-colored reading chair.

I've thought to leave a note for Mr. Goring, who is about the fifth Londoner who has gone into a semi (but only a semi, mind you) panic upon hearing that I am in analytic-training.

My remark to him is "Don't worry—if I'm not getting paid I'm not working!"

That ought to set his mind at ease—but is it true?

No. My brain thinks about people in a psychoanalytic way almost all the time.

We were in Southern Warwickshire this weekend, visiting an English family we met in the Athens airport. A doctor, his 33 year-old lawyer son, and his stepmother! Wow—what a study that was! Oh—and their lipstick-colored cat. (Well anyway, I've got a cat-colored lipstick, rosy apricot by Chanel, precisely matched the unusual color of this chubby friendly bourgeois country cat.)

I begin with our return flight from London in April 1983, as I mused upon the time during which Hubby became acquainted with the principals and the problems of his case, and I got acquainted with glorious London again. It ends, for all intents and purposes, on February 10, 1986, with the decision from the judge, mostly but not entirely favorable to our side.

BAKING IN BAKERSFIELD

Culmination to many a glamorous deposition sight—Bakersfield. The main kernel of Kern County, California. Center of U.S. almond production, home of big oil interests, above all of agribusiness. Hubby living outside of Bakersfield while trying a case having to do with just such an agricultural caper. Me flying along the byways and flyways coming up to see him.

June 21—the last evening, longest day of the year. I love that summer solstice. Flying up in my car, I say flying because of the ascension and descension I witness curiously from the almost living room-like comfort of my front seat. All I had to do was steer occasionally. The car was on cruise control and practically drove itself through the tawny wheat and green meadows. I kept the speedometer cautiously at 61 M.P.H. since it was an enormous temptation to do my favorite trick, which is to accelerate up the mountains and then put the car into neutral to sail down them again, picking up enormous amounts of speed and saving huge amounts of gasoline—I always think. Mostly I did not because passing Taft and Maricopa reminded me of a hugely expensive speeding ticket I once got playing this game about twelve years ago in another trial situation in Bakersfield. It's very tempting—the highways are architectural masterpieces. One can hug any lane of the eight lane causeway while banking and in my heavy car, I sail almost effortlessly along. I drank in the wonderful non-L.A. scenery. I'm so tired of almost three months of dirty, hazy L.A. days and raw thickly throated acrid air. I'm sick of air I can see and what's more—smell and taste. It's like a chemical dump—the whole of the metropolitan area. Even our supposed upper class, west side environs. We are not Pomona or Glendale but it is plenty bad enough for my respiratory system to cope with. So I love it when after an hour of driving, the air lets me see detail of rock, brush and tree that are blurred and blunted in the city. The territory north so alternately Africa-like, stark and tawny and precipitously mountainous and rocky, quite respectable size lakes hold their own with Switzerland: Castaic, Hughes, and Isabella. I love driving up this way because of the unfamiliarity—the route to Palm Springs and San Diego are boringly familiar by now. I love being out in the sticks. I love some of the turn-off signs coming here—*Weed Patch Three Miles, Run Away Truck Ramp Two Miles Ahead, Severe Dust Warning for Next 40 Miles, Last Gas Before Mojave Desert, Tejon Pass 4400 Feet, Comanche Drive, Pumpkin Patch.* This is a boil-over stretch now, large rigs start reeking with gas fumes. Huge trucks steaming from the hood, many unfortunate vacationers pull disconsolately off the side of the road while listless and dejected cats and dogs see their plans for the day go down the drain or up in smoke, rather. It's tough on motors—the grapevine. I imagine these huge passes through the San Gabriel Mountains are called Grapevine because they bring the traveler from coastal L.A. to the areas of the inland empire, the magnificent San Joaquin Valley which grows a lot of grape.

It's true that terrorists have again taken hostages and San Diego may be trembling again on the verge of the big one—lots and lots of small temblors seem to presage this—but up here at the Rio Bravo Country Club, all that seems a world away. In fact, I'm plunged back in memory to a swimming place we frequented in Williamsport, Pennsylvania. I had little to do then, those summer days as I do now, but hang around, reading and writing at the pool, spending an hour lazily making my way up and down the huge pool, rocking with Middle American youth, mostly blond Bakersfieldians. Many with crew or modified punk cuts, shouting and laughing in the pool, many handsome Asians sprinkled amongst them, Japanese, Chinese and yes, lots of Mexicans; newly middle class in fact, last Saturday's wedding was of a splendidly tall, blond Anglo Saxon to a small Mexican girl. This is June—there is a fresh bridal party here every Saturday. It is a pleasant site for a nuptial. During the day, I don't notice the heat so much. Last weekend's 107 didn't faze me much during the day because mostly I'm either in the pool or drying off from my swim, or about to reenter the 60' by 200' turquoise treat. This is quite an oasis between the desert and the Sierra Nevada Range. It quite agrees with me, the sun soothes and comforts my aches and pains. All the body exertions in the warm waters of the huge pool leave me feeling sleepy and smugly sunned as a chameleon. My return from here to L.A. last Monday made me feel quite Mary Queen of Scots-like. Isolation, gloom, gray, cold. The days may be 80ish and breezy, but nights are 57 and dank, dank, dank after the desert. Arthritis creeps into my joints and bones on little wasped feet, stinging and swelling as it goes. As I turned in to 178 East last night on the final lap of the 2-1/4 hour trip from home, the heat all but smothered me. At night, I am in dry clothes and I feel it so much more than I do in my wet swimsuit. Fun, though, like a cross between Lawrence of Arabia and Death Valley West. People are ever so much more friendly here than in the big city. So interested in who and what we are. Friendly country people feeling extremely sophisticated at their Rio Bravo Country Club. This is the big time around here. Just like Texas; well-to-do folks, maybe even oil rich, with real down home ways. Folksy and friendly. I cannot decide whether or not to take seriously my psychoanalytic career and schooling. So different from the counseling field I've come from. In psychoanalysis the treatment gives no advice, no suggestions, no judgments, no behavior modification, and no homework. What do we give—our attention, our fifty minute session, our comments on the resistance and the transference and our interpretations, but those like measured doses of strong medicine—not to be thrown around lightly, but to be savored. My style is now somewhere between the two schools. It is virtually impossible for me to be that pure; one is only human, of course, and loves to intermeddle sometimes. Dinner is not until 8:30 p.m.—I'm starved. Got a Snickers bar out of the machine by the pool—it's a waxed packet of melted down peanut goop. Forgot the machine is also sitting in 100 degree heat. With the sprinkling system pulsing morning and night, some beautiful conifers and aspens flourish around the generous balcony. Their leaves are quaking with the early evening desert hot breezes. Colors are so vivid out of L.A., it's like someone looking around after a cataract operation. No more blur. The fewer the people, the more precious each one seems. There is something to be said for small towns, particularly if they are fairly close to big ones. You can big fish it all week, and get revived on the weekend by a plunk or two in a big pond. Back and forth I ply on weekends.

SECOND BAKERSFIELD WEEKEND

I start out at the same time as before—7:15 p.m. on a Friday afternoon. This time, the sky is feathered with gray clouds and a bit bleak, but what a sunset this engenders. The air becomes dramatic at about Saugus, visibly crispened and degunked. Just as dramatic a change as driving from Pacific Palisades into town—the gray fog lightens predictably at a certain street, maybe 26th, at a certain hill or turn on Sunset. From the soup to the sweet sun. The ominous gray proceeds to a vulgar cerise, if not for the fringes or blue-gray which interdigitate and sober it up, it would be garish. If the changing colors go on and on for over a half hour, by the time I'm over the grapevine again (which I love) and straining to see the last lovely tissues of pink, I'm in the flatlands.

The vanilla scented oleander trees (even if their leaves do poison babies) I usually enjoy in the center of the freeway, but now they've become a real barrier as I curse them for looming up between me and the symphony of color finale-ing over distant Bakersfield to the left. Absolutely rats, cheated, can't see it anymore as 99 pulls me from the clouds to the clods. Like leaving the hall before the concert climaxes. The heat assaults me at this point. I have to put on air conditioning even though it's night now. This is unheard-of behavior for me. Finding my way more and more around this area which I've come to love, tawny hills give way to superbly Alpine scenery on 178 up a winding gorge to Lake Isabella. Beautiful green, white water of the heretofore unknown to me Kern River. The color of the Saltz River in Austria, the only truly emerald river I'd ever seen before. Massive granite outcroppings, a sculpture garden that extends for 100 miles, then flattens out to Lake Isabella. Then around the loops to the astonishing Tahatchapi area, full of changes and surprises up and around the rolling, hilly areas, with valleys that change their content about every third valley. One full of Joshua trees just finished blooming, white petals still drifting across the road—now that's exotic. Other valleys full of grass and lucky cattle grazing, others full of plain old tumbleweed, very Wyoming-like. Others full of windmills, producing electrical power. This area is really country. Radio gets only country and western stations. Folks at markets, gas stations, ranch houses, dispensing homemade pie and homemade soups. The ranch houses are filled with interesting, humorous, and above all, very down-home types. Couldn't dispense more homely wisdom and folksy fussing if they were Minnie Pearl with the price tag hanging in her face. Are they "for real"? I think so. There's not terribly much to do indoors around here but keep themselves amused with their own humor. I was finally able to really test drive my car and let it go flat out up to 110 M.P.H. on a desert stretch. Gorgeous, never loved my glorious car so much as when it could do that speed and feel smooth and unflustered as at 30 M.P.H. Don't tell the C.H.P. though. Rather stunned by my service station attendant who has expressed a good deal of contempt that I've never taken it up and broken it in, but how can you on a C.H.P. loaded freeway—but out in the desert, that's another story…speedier and better. It will be a different black and white story going back up this holiday weekend, the 4th of July weekend. Half of America will be headed for the Sierra Nevadas and I won't be able to let it out on the flats I'm sure. I'm going to investigate the way to pick up police signals. I just heard there was such a thing. If there are any officers reading this, hum, fat chance, I'm a small blond person with bouffant hair and look a bit like Dolly Parton driving a diesel rig, of course. Actually, I am enjoying a real honeymoon period with my XJ6. I've never felt strongly about cars or mechanical things other than being relieved when they aren't breaking down and needing to be in the shop. Always at 8:00 a.m. in the morning, of course, when I'm catching a couple of ZZZ's or valiantly battling to write down my dreams for my analytic session. I don't want to put the kibosh on my kiddie-car, but I've waited two years next week to give it a rousing 'well done!" or if "kineahora" sounds good, go for it.

Actually, you don't have to be Jewish to love Yiddish. Most moxy folks, especially in showbiz know lots more than I do. Anyway, my little pal has been 100% of a lady so far, and takes a 6% grade and gusty wind conditions beautifully as her breeding would lead you to expect. The tougher the grade, the more this buggy shows what it's made of. I'm so glad to have something with a fine pedigree; God knows the rest of us don't have anything nearly as illustrious in our backgrounds. No horse thieves but no arch dukes either. Mostly just Russian mediocrities with my maternal grandfather starring as the intellectual, having been a pharmacist in the Port of Odessa at the turn of the century and having a letter to the editor printed in *The New York Times* as well. No small satisfaction for someone mastering English in his third decade of life.

In case you don't know it, Bakersfield is the fastest growing city in California. Forget silicon chips, think water, think cotton, melons, grapes, oil, its lovely-close to gorgeous-wilderness country. The people look to be of Anglo Saxon stock, fairheaded, attractive, friendly, much like in manners and mores of the America of my youth. People go out of their way to be funny, friendly and helpful. Case in point - a young man in a local locksmith store across from the main post office at G & Eye Street in Bakersfield spent more than an hour in the blazing sun fitting key molds into my locked trunk. Finally, a very much unexpected one worked. I had to have that trunk opened-most young guys would have worked a little while and said "Sorry, we haven't got the right key" which was the truth but it was the sheer perseverance that worked. Good man, Adam. There are, of course, obviously large Asian populations-with wonderful Szechuan and Mandarin Restaurants everywhere to serve them-and obvious Mexican folks. Most unusual are the Basques, an ancient people much given to barque building (see the recent *National Geographic Magazine* that says Basque barques dating from prehistoric times have been preserved and are being carbon-dated). They are also much given to sheepherding and cooking lamb in a zillion ways. Love the restaurants, Wool Growers, Chalet Basque and some others. Where you get family style, fresh tomatoes, pickled tongue, vegetable soup with salsa, and beans to put in it, overcooked green beans is the only minus item, and love those prices. They are half of what a great fresh meal costs in Los Angeles. The Mexican food offered up at the Red Pepper off Oswell Street, out to the northeast on the way to the Rio Bravo Lodge, also serves a meal I like. Very fresh vegetable soup with some tiny cumin and garlic spiced meatballs at the bottom of the large bowl which you ladle out yourself. Then the nicely dressed mild crunchy salad. Next, my favorite, camarones a la española, followed by a good flan. Lots of margaritas, chips, salsa and Dos Equis abound on the table (but not in front of my place). If you keep on 178 east after leaving the Red Pepper, you will wind your way past Leons, my staff of life, near the lodge. They have refrigerators full of good egg or tuna salad sandwiches, and are open seven days a week, 24 hours a day. Campers, stock car fans and anglers, river rafters and softball players keep those sandwiches turning over. The Rio Bravo pleasant big pool, zillions of tennis courts and very large comfy rooms, hot-hot in July but clean dry air. Oh, and a baby llama lives between Leon's and the lodge. He is small, alone and looks utterly out of place in a Bakersfield corral, his next-door neighbor is a baby calf. I am meaning before this case is over to find out why and who he is, and why he is not summering in the Andes where he belongs instead of blistering in cow and horse country. I bet he has a fascinating past. Perhaps he is a hostage from a highjack on a flight from Lima. My husband and I are enduring our longest separation since army days in 1956-58. I trust him, but I've told him one false move up there when I'm trustingly keeping things going down here, and his delicate shell collection gets trashed... and I mean it, it'll be sand when I'm done with it if he doesn't behave.

OJAI

Missed the Greek Festival in the park in Santa Barbara, missed driving to the Reagan ranch or toward it anyway, and missed visiting the old Olive Mill this visit. To make up for the limited number of experiences we could encompass in one weekend, I took a brand new route home and that was an adventure. Instead of heading straight down the coast; I turned inland past Carpenteria toward Ojai, with winding rural countryside but very chic, an occasional farm but mostly gentlemen and ladies growing avocados and citrus to supplement their main revenue, which means clipping coupons or maintaining one's portfolio. Ojai is incontestably up-market. If you don't have inherited trust funds, you'd better be a renowned ceramicist or an internationally known miniaturist at the very least. A while ago, we visited one artist who had an entire mandarin court complete with diminutive ceremonial kimonos and long, jeweled, curved, lacquered, and menacing fingernails to show who was and who was not the peon around there. Before Ojai, I drove by Castaic Lake Park—very lovely, clean and deserted. Out the other side of Ojai, I started climbing and weaving through some very tough mountains, deeply precipitous as Tahiti or Kauai. Dozens of hairpin turns to negotiate. Later I emerged back down in the flatlands.

STYLE HALLOWEEN OCTOBER 31

First it was Rambo. Then it was Banana Republic. Then the sublime Meryl Streep in *Out of Africa.*

What was, you ask? Why, I reply, the sartorial climate that accounts for my running the streets looking like an urban Che Guevara. All right, all right, I exaggerate. I look like the somewhat portly lady I am, visiting her husband in Century City dressed in this season's alternative to denim (*le serge de Nimes*) mufti! Actually I look a lot like my husband when he went out to play war games in the fields around Fort Hood, when we were in Texas for his basic training. In 1956. 32 years ago.

This green, brown, and spotted stuff began to be seen on TV when we first sent troops as advisors to the Central American jungles. The style caught on and was extended to army troops on home soil. Soon, little boys demanded to wear it too, and moms dressed their tots in camouflage to go to the playground. Mufti became more and more chic; soon it hit Beverly Hills and the brat pack. Then…Neiman Marcus for the under-size 10, fresh from the *Jane Fonda's Workout* bunch. By the time it gets adopted by the Lane Bryant crowd, you know it's establishment city.

None the less, I'm having a good time padding around Gelsons, Westwood, and other dangerous rebel outposts in my khaki pants with cargo pockets, khaki shirt with military tabs on the shoulders, camouflage jacket and visored cap.

Fancying myself as romantic, dashing....hoping maybe the casual observer will mistake me for a game warden from the Serengeti. Or a delegate with a peace mission from Panama. Or maybe a romantic sabra fresh from assignment guarding a remote outpost in the Golan Heights.

I'm not too sure I'm fooling anyone though. Somehow I still just look like me and it's Halloween time. Actually, my hat and jacket have great sentimental value; they were bought at the Woolrich store which is halfway between my old hometown of Williamsport, Pennsylvania and ye old Alma Mater, Penn State, and were probably devised so the deer hunters can sneak up on the deer while pretending to be forest, sort of like an American Burnham Woods.

Anyway, it gives me a certain identification with my past, and hunters stalking through the blazing autumn Appalachians. It recalls the bite of a crisp apple and the smell of black leafy nights in my Williamsport childhood. I loved to scamper though the streets of this town of 60,000 souls on Halloween night, thrilled and scared to be out on the streets in the dark, but basically safe and sound as a bug in a rug in the nights of the 1930's. No chain saw murderers, no razor blades in candies or satanic Sabbaths threatened in those days. Children were everyone's concern, and adults were mostly parental, the occasional loony was locked up tight in the jailhouse before he could do much damage.

Not so here in L.A. in 1987...there are a plethora of weird people camping out on corners of Hollywood, and in our western suburbs, the homeless vie with denizens from the V.A. for a doorway. There are so many mentally ill on the streets!—frightening wigs, outfits and makeup seem to be redundant. It just doesn't seem to be safe enough out there to risk attracting attention to oneself. So my only concession to the time of year, besides baby pumpkins and dry Indian corn on the dining room table as a centerpiece, is my little joke of an outfit.

The joke part is that probably no army in the world would find me fit enough to wear my paratrooper jumpsuit in earnest. It's a lot like the little jogging suits and shoes for newborns, just a way to be part of the crowd, but not really a player.

California started with tennis clothes on ladies who never went to the courts, but just wanted their neighbors to think they could if they wanted. Well, that's how I feel about my little get-up; it gives me options.

Isn't all dress up that way anyway, an attempt to fill out in fantasy what most of us lack in reality?

(The most in costume this season in my crowd by far and away is the tuxedo. Formerly reserved for Academy Award presenters and nominees, now formal attire is affected by the non-rich and non-famous as well. Los Angelenos have watched too much *Dynasty* I fear; folks are slipping into their monkey suits for almost any occasion whatsoever. Back yard barbeques. Lox and bagel brunches. Sailboat rides around the Marina on a Sunday afternoon. Soon everyone will own their own tuxedo, but until that happens, it is still "I have one and you don't, so there!" time. Every man his own Gatsby. Every man his own Swell.)

My uniform is my little tribute to those blowy nights long ago when only children acted out their scenarios on the streets, the grown-ups waited for private parties to appear childish. Otherwise they remained cloaked in business suits and house-dresses under aprons. In the 30's, I assure you, right after the real depression, not this mirage of a one; anyone over 16 wanted to look respectable and solid, as if he or she could hold a good-paying job and be an asset to his company. No one craved to look kinky, unshaven or even especially sexy…America's business was business. For all the rest, one could go to the movies and bask in Hollywood's ideas of glamour, adventure and daring-do.

Now, everyone gives themselves the license to live it out, if not in the 9 to 5 world, at least after-hours. Last month, we saw a new-style motorcycle gang on Melrose Avenue. I swear all the young men were either stockbrokers or young lawyers out of Harvard. You never saw such good looks and excellent grooming in your life. The girls looked to be out of finishing schools by way of a Hell's Angels internship.

Even the punks are not usually out to mug you and grab your purse, they are generally just graduating from hair dressing school and wanting to try out their Do's. Or waiting for their SAT scores so they can apply to a good college. But there is just enough real menace on the streets so you don't know for sure who is who, that is why costume seems a bit redundant now.

And *that* is why little old ladies wear combat boots and fatigues. To keep all you tricksters on your toes.

BAKERSFIELD—THE RIO BRAVO

Once again, I am privy to a slice of privileged life in a little known and out of the way spot here in the heartland of Bakersfield, the northeast corner just beyond the flat farmlands, just before the climb along the tumbling Kern River, on Highway 178 East, climbing 3,000 feet to Lake Isabella. There are some really, really nice granite overlooks at strategic points to sit and observe the tumbling gray-green waters. Anyway, at this outpost of leisure, the Rio Bravo Lodge, one can speculate about the style of upwardly aspiring and already aspirated folks enjoying fresh air, good golf and smashing tennis amidst low rolling puppy-beige foothills; and superb, delicious air to breathe and very sweet fresh water to drink straight from the tap; delicacies unavailable at any price in Los Angeles.

Anyway, I am up delivering some T.L.C. to Hubby beleaguered under ten tons of files pertaining to crazy top, hardpan, June drop and various kinds of dripping, squirting, leaking, flooding and malfunctioning sprinkler systems all involved in his big case against some allegedly fraudulent almond growers in Kern County and a big Chicago bank. Although outposted at this lovely lodge, life has not been a bowl of well, salted almonds, for him in the last half year. For the last five months during the trial, he has survived temperatures upwards of 110 degrees Fahrenheit, searing droughts that leave a litigator's throat dry as a crispy critter, dust storms and wildcat fires that have licked the very road circumnavigating the lodge itself, not to mention bought experts (are there any other kind?), renegade witnesses and the bane of all banes-phlegm in the throat. More dreaded than this and not even to be thought of as he goes into his closing argument next Monday and Tuesday is *laryngitis.*

Anyway, in this oasis of country club type life, there is a nice looking young kid who hoses down the tennis courts full time. You could eat off them, they're so clean. How upper class can you get? He does this chore, by the way, in the most preppy of preppy tennis clothes. The people at the Rio Bravo, all over the town of Bakersfield for that matter, are very interested and concerned, anxious to please, to be of help and service. Fern at the front desk for instance, charming, funny, unpretentious, and slender as a young girl. Waitresses all over would be admired by Mable Morgan lovers everywhere. Bee-hive hair and very sweet-natured. Hard by this oasis of civility, however, we find the barbarians sniffing at the gates.

Circumnavigating the lodge and grounds is a road leading to Ming Lake. The landscape is black and dead due to fires consuming the sparse brown cover. Along this black space are beer bottles and cans, thrown contemptuously by the bikers who go past and congregate at Hart Park.

TREKKIES FOREVER

You bet! Just blew out of *Star Trek Five* and I'm happy to say: Bones is bonier than ever, Navigator Spock more Mephistophelean than ever, and Captain Kirk has managed to keep his gut down to manageable dimensions. Over and above all this, the guys certainly are all aging... but still hanging right in there, and thank your lucky pajamas for that! Oh yes, the regulation Starfleet P.J.s have been pleasingly updated, and have many more tailoring details about them.

Yes, the entire original cast has all managed to stay alive, for which I personally, as well as generically, am very thankful. Our eldest son went to U.E.S. (University Elementary School) with the Nimoy boy, and later went to Berkeley undergrad with Shatner's daughter, so the old fleet commanders are about the same age as Hubby and me; we are happy to see that these adventurers into the unknown still know enough about our current planet to take their intergalactic Geritol and visit their extraterrestrial nutritionists as well.

Yep, all is well with the Enterprise family, and the plot of this new one is quite fascinating. The gang are off to meet God, no less. Yessiree-bob, that is thinking big. I am relieved to say we are not getting into any Oral Roberts-Tammy Faye Baker kind of stuff. Gene Rodenberry is too liberal and sane for that! (After a week of seeing right-wing crazies blocking abortion clinics and tearing each other to bits for a shred of the Ayatollah's shroud, I've had just about enough of the religious right wing, thank you very much.) In fact, those scenes are almost enough to make me turn against *anyone's* religion.

The movie was a pastiche of all the great shtick from recent films, so there are echoes, in the desert world of the opening scene, of Peter O'Toole meeting Omar Sharif in *Lawrence of Arabia.* Next, a flashback to the bar scene out of *Star Wars*, complete with woggies, spooks, klingons, mutants and animals of various persuasions. We have the breakthrough of the "great barrier" between the natural and the supernatural worlds, a spin off of *2001* if I ever saw one, complete with the requisite swirling matter-cum-tunnel, and an arrival scene on the new planet. Then comes the encounter with God... if that wasn't an update of the *Wizard of Oz* as rendered by Frank Morgan and explained in Psychoanalysis 101, I'll just be a monkey's uncle…

See, god (ahem God) appears in a sort of holograph projected on the sky and undoubtedly sound crafted by Lucas sound labs. At first, the crew thinks this is the real thing, a powerful dude indude, I mean indeed. But when "god" announces he must have the starship to broadcast the news that he exists, the good guys begin to get a *little suspicious* about why god needs a star ship if he is God, for heavens sake. Then the quasi-villain quasi-vulcan, half brother of Lieutenant Spock or Commander Spock…I'm a little hazy about his rank… realizes that this god is some kind of a sensual projection of his very own psyche, that "god" is himself writ hugely large and loud on the canvas of eternity. Who we are, and who we then expect to see, is the basis of this massive theatrical projective identification. And he doesn't much like it; no, he does not…

Joseph Campbell, you were right all along. If there really is no such thing as god, we then are forced to invent one. For man must have his myths and his beliefs to survive...and to justify…this journey we call our life.

Although '*Trek*' is quite the collage of every flick that ever grossed big bucks or big yucks at the box office, it combined the recognizable bits with enough pizazz that even old Trekkies like me were enchanted.

Did I forget to tell you about Spock playing Superman? Well, he did, and in his turbo-boots at that, he hovers over the face of El Capitan-to save his buddy Kirk from a possibly nasty fall off the Yosemite landmark. That's right, Kirk is intrepid even in a state park. They've topped themselves off with an Ansell Adams bit… I tell you, they haven't missed trick one.

The denouement? Kirk says it all, there ain't nothing Out There; whatever there is, is inside here...us humans that is. God, the real god, does not force people, does not take hostages, and does not steal, threaten, conjure, cajole or play lotto.

So how was the movie, really? It was swell, it was great, I can't wait to see it again, and where can I buy one of those spiffy outfits for myself?

Us true Trekkies hesitate not to go where no man has gone before! Back to Westwood...to pay top dollar for a dynamite new *Star Trek*, and may numbers six, seven and eight be close behind, and the crew double up on their Geritol for the coming efforts.

PARTICLES, BOMBS AND THEORIES

I learned it at Cal Tech, there was a young man from Peking who did some very deep profound thinking. This man by the name of Yao found a teensy particle...somehow a trillionth the size of an electron. We won't be able to verify his calculations, for no technology exists for this super-duper micro world. I am not even remotely qualified to make any statement to prove or disprove this theory; I am positively defunct in the non-verbal dimensions (I never got the same answer twice in second grade math.) I still don't! These Yao manifolds come under the Aegis of String theory which is not thought of as being nearly so mathematically correct as quantum mechanics, which has been repeatedly measured to be accurate to one part in ten billion, making it the most successful physical theory of all time. Scientists, mostly male, trying to understand the nature of matter at its smallest scale: Quantum mechanics, Particle physics, the atom bomb, the neutron bomb, the particle bomb. But now there are gluons and muons, and don't give a hoo-on. And did you know the heaviest particle ever found? It is a quark bound up with its anti-quark. Also, a lepton as well as its antiparticle equals the Tau Lepton. It is *very* heavy, I thought we were down to the limit with science right up to the minute. I wonder what about the very elusive Higgs particle that is supposed, like molasses, to provide mass to the empty space that makes up the structure of the cosmos.

How come if space is so empty I seem to take up so much of it? Do you think that space is full of matter? Well if you were looking at an atom as a football stadium, the stadium would be empty. Since the nucleus would be the size of a grain of sand. How come if space is so empty, my clothes are feeling so tight on me? All of this will be revealed by data rolling out from CERN; analyzed, collated and interpreted by the folks at The Large Hadron Collider, which is set up to find answers for such sundry small jobs as finding the origin of the universe (big bang). The Higgs Boson? Don't even mention "god" Richard Dawkins would have a fit! And with that waiver.... I will quit. Bye bye birdies.

It's the end of summer here in Smog City. If that were not ominous enough, I have suddenly turned into a middle age menace to the ecosystem. Move over, Ludvig.

How can this happen to a good guy like me, one who supports critters and habitat from the gulfstream to Glacier Bay?

Like this: in early March, I planted some two dozen half-inch high sprigs of assorted cosmos, knowing this would solve my color problem through the hot months to come. I knew they would grow, and tried to be cautious with my purchase from Mordigan's Nursery, whose stock does flourish, but I was intrigued with the tiny ferns breaking through and purchased a whole flat, instead of a half-flat, as a part of me knew I should.

Well, daisies and foxglove and delphinium came and went all spring. Tiny ferns basking in their drip-system, and fresh fertilizers proliferated everywhere. In June, the first pink, white and magenta flowers appeared, and it's been a wild carnival of color ever since. The plants have long since overwhelmed their 2' by 4' stakes from Armstrong's, and trampled every petunia under stems that grew to the thickness of succulents...maybe I did too good a job preparing the soil.

Along with the ferniness and profuse blossoms came a rainforest full of fast, round olive- colored birds that twittered in the cosmos bushes like parrots in the canopies of 100 foot trees. They swayed on the twigs, munched on the petals, and roistered with their fellows. The strange part about these creatures is that though they come when I plant cosmos, I never see them out of cosmos season, either here or anywhere else that I have looked.

This year I determined to find out what they were. According to *Fielding's Guide to Birds of Southern California*, they look most like the page of warblers. They have either yellow or white markings, they are about the right size, chubby 6 inchers, and seem to behave in the darting way of warblers of legend.

Easy? Not really. Puzzling. A-Why are they in a book about California, when they are found either in Nicaragua, or in the case of the Baltimore Warbler, Maryland? What, they got in on the price wars the airlines are running till October lst? That's a hell of a lot more than I can do. Anywhere I want to go, its full-fare plus, due to the erratic nature of Hubby's trial lawyering...crowded court calendars, over jammed court systems etc. They seem too little to wing it up on their own petal power. And just where are they when they are not confounding the population of Brentwood, and what do they eat?

I endlessly enjoy their morning and evening forays into the thickets of summery foliage, which take place in full view of the sliding glass doors off the kitchen...and have for months and months, as promised. However, the plants they depend on are dying, according to which bloomed first, so the large lush pink ones in the right hand corner are about bald. Others straggle and drunkenly lean away from decent containing. The party is certainly over for at least half of the miniature ecosystem, but how to manage the birds and still spruce up the garden, which looks like the old Collier brothers home everything saved, nothing in order?

I devise a scheme, to save the environment for the birds and hope they don't notice a *gradual* clearing process, taking out the moribund but leaving those plants that can provide play and grocery supplies. With heart in mouth, as more and more warblers seem to accumulate in a tizzy at breakfast and dinnertime, as if to say, "Hello to all and enjoy our company, I may give the orders to Ricardo my cosmos hit man. "Take out every other one, leave the ones with flowers."

It's done, the old cleared out, pathetic bare spots. At six, there are six olive-backed and lemon-tummied critters sitting on a branch of the overhanging lemon tree, turning their heads to one another and twittering very rapidly. What the hell happened here, a nuclear drop? Who would do this to us, is it a state of all-out war? Do we get our visas now?

I am smitten with guilt. They are not eating. They are not flying. They are pow-wowing. They no longer trust their environment, and move off together in a cloud for the neighbor's peach tree, long bare of peaches, to commune some more. I feel punished. It was not worth it. I share my anguish with Hubby, who shrugs his shoulders and allows, "That's life in the big city."

There are dark red and white bushes left, but evidently the little beasts love only the pink. I think they hate what the uprooting has done to the overcrowded, but previously at least somewhat landscaped garden. For a while they sulk next door. Next day they winged through, smelled…or seemed to smell the white and the red specimens, and landed next door. On strike.

Slowly but surely, in ones and twos, they are returning. They frisk again in the one big bush, but no longer fly near the kitchen door to say hi. Move over, Saddam Hussein.

I don't think I can bear another Hobson's choice like this next summer. I'm considering not planting any cosmos, vacationing in Nicaragua, going xerioscape and letting cactus prevail. Doing all my bird watching at the aviary section of the L.A. Zoo.

GETTING THERE

Well today–I'm sitting in a strange gazebo in a strange land gazing at a body of water I've never even heard of. The islands are the Yasaba chain; the sea is Coral; the Island Laucaula (pronounced Lau-thala). It belongs to Malcolm Forbes. The water is teeming with strange fish; our end of the island is deserted except for the "people who take care of us."

My ontogeny cannot wait or recapitulate this phylogeny!

I'm out of the sun now in a little thatched oceanside gazebo, shady, and breezy.

After the misery of the waiting room at the airport, even though first class and luxurious, the sound of the people's shrill chatter and coughing; the relentlessness of their cigarette smoke in my lungs almost driving me mad—on top of extreme fatigue and inhuman frustration.

The trip was costing a fortune and everything that could go amuck—was. Weather, airlines, taxis, connections, all mis-firing.

Now this primeval and unnamed ocean laps at the gazebo. The peace of it! The sound is healing. There are no other guests.

Erica/Isadora Jong needs her dream-she loves to get through angst to peace. The fleshly reunion—uniting process precedes the spiritual ecstasy.

Hubby and I get this after reunion with our primal environment, the salty seas of the world.

Creatures that have floated in a sea of salt nutrient for nine months need to revisit their environmental crèche from time to time.

If I never have one more person blow smoke in my face, I'll be happy alone forever (with four in help) and with the seaside smells.

Our shelling guide, Mere, has features that betray her aboriginal origins. Her people clearly sailed to these Yasaba Islands from New Guinea, perhaps. Or Australia. Or New Zealand. She looks part Maori—part aboriginal, as does her son.

Only a small enclave in Fiji is pure Polynesian looking. There are also many exotic mixtures.

This is a copra plantation inland; there are workers and their children. There is a cook and a maid, and two boat staff. (One, Suli, to sail and the other, Mere, to get into the water with us and find shells. Also to shake her head *no!* when something we think is cute is also poisonous. I picked up a darling black ruffles sea slug; she shook her head hard and looked alarmed—I dropped it!)

There are no other guests. The sea lulls me with its primal murmur. I've yearned for this sound.

Uncontaminated with squeals, sirens, screams, and the Grateful Dead.

There's a piece of coral at my feet, a dead ringer for a shark fin—a marine look-alike. The ocean still holds plenty of mysteries for me—not only coral sharks, and the droplet—size squads of fish that rise from time to time on the surface of the water—like an inverse rain squall. I've seen them flying in the Caribbean—there, they even have long transparent pectorals–half fins, half wings to help them.

Lots of action under the bland surface; now it's 4:15 pm. There must be Escher eating Escher fish down there—for small and large fish plop up, and splash singularly down again. A torrent of one. Clearly something is planning to dine on them; this *tour jete* is nature's tool for them to choreograph their survival.

Whoops, something new toward the dock. A group of flashing silver beings rising—*then skipping in formation* again and again to show their dozens of bodies in perfect formation. At the same time, a large silver fish takes to the air near them—but going in the opposite direction.

I am positive there are entities in waters still undreamed about. Not only Loch Ness types, but smaller and undreamed of beings. We've just discovered tons of life forms living where they cannot live–in the dark. In the deep. We haven't been to the bottoms of our chasms—we've only begun to search the sides and throw a dim beam or two here and there for one or two blinks.

Got a great idea for proper aquatic attire from our boat-lady who gets in the water in her sundress.

No one's around. I detest swimsuits—they are tight and itchy with elastic and spandex when new—and a torment when wet and sandy. Evidently, this five o'clock time is cocktail hour everywhere—because single fish are Baryshnikov-ing their way up and hopefully out of the way in scores of places right now. Like a big skin is being drawn around them. Or a very hot iron pan is smoking with fresh butter for the evening sauté.

There are little rollings and boilings beneath the surface, but odd to say—no birds at all at, or near, or above these waters teeming, trust me, with the flashing doom.

Oh yes, I've decided to enter, exit, and swim in a short muumuu which I can easily peel off for a dry muumuu! Hooray!

I tell you, the sea is now *alive* with the pescadores doing, in teams or solo, *A Chorus Line* or star turn, Nijinsky or Radio City Music Hall, jumping, flying, skipping, or eating.

But damn—I've got to leave my pristine perch. The bugs are starting to swarm; news is out on the Fijian Archipelago that fresh meat from L.A. is served—not even contaminated by Honolulu saliva (too cold for mosquitoes or summer clothes). Oh oh, got to run to the shower, there's sand in my scalp and the no-see-us are chewing on me like *crazy*.

Ah—cool shower—I soak under it gratefully—use some of the Wella special shampoo on the ledge. Malcolm Forbes? His magazines are everywhere—why not?

One second to shampoo, and ten minutes to rinse—water is so *soft* the lather keeps coming and coming. Um—into two large pale blue towels. There are piles and piles of them everywhere. Then, onto the terry bedspread to rest. Um—skin soothed—will need a lot of unguents and Neosporin for tootsies sorely scraped when I tried to climb out of some rocks back into the boat.

Oh, did John Updike write transcendentally—definitely about his skin? Its extra layers and defoliation in *At War With My Skin* in *The New Yorker.* About my favorite piece by him, one of my three current favorites, along with Erica Jon and Russell Baker.

The lines are the size of the papayas. The papayas are as big as footballs. There are fresh coconuts festooning trees around us, ready to divulge with some luscious juice—and/or nowadays give me a concussion.

It will be muumuus for me forever if I don't watch the calorie intake. Everything with a waist stays in my suitcase—bring on the clowns!

SPRING 1986

It's spring. I do want to go to Ft. Lauderdale and boogie, but I don't want to get out, out, out into nature.

On Mondays, I start appointments late. I hopped into my car and purred luxuriously up the San Diego Freeway, and east on the Ventura. I've had my nose inside my book for so long. I looked around at the new leaves like a prisoner released from a life sentence in jail. Anything would have looked gorgeous to me in my two hours of blessed freedom; but today it is lovely, the San Fernando Valley, surrounded by sweet, cool mountains, completely capped with snow from the storms. Clear going east, but clouded up an hour-and-a-half later. The trip inland was incredible. I had my car stereo turned to 90.5 F.M., an invigorating Stravinsky selection, it was beautiful. My jag drove magnificently. I felt like I was surveying the Himalayas from Katmandu. How's that for feeling exotic? My mini-vacation state-of-mind was taking me. Far away indeed.

The zoo's parking lot was mostly empty except for four school buses. It was easy to avoid the school children. I have to go on days when I can pretend I really am out in the wild. First of all, the L.A. Zoo has a wonderful new entryway full of shops and ice cream parlors, and attractive boutiques all done in a warm salmon and turquoise that reminds one of the Olympic colors and that high time—when L.A. was at its best. We were on a high, the airport worked and we were proud of our city. People around the world wanted to move here and enjoy its glories. (Actually, I think they all have, judging from the usual condition of the freeway.)

I made for the baby zoo, which had some darling infant lowland monkeys rolling about-touching their white wooly blankets, or maybe they were sheepskins—for all the world like little New Zealand babies, except goats, and a scrawny infant lemur. So I set briskly up the path, carefully by-passing the seal and polar bear sections, too familiar and well-worn. Hung a left at the pretty-faced wallabies, and realized this was the first time I'd been to the down-under section of the zoo since my return from Australia in January. Really noticed the large gray kangaroos, the silky-furred wallabies, and the knotty-topped cassowary birds, like giant emus or ostriches with wicked and huge feet. Wow—that could open up an eye in a flash with no trouble at all. Strange creatures. From New Guinea. I'd like to go there someday.

I walked briskly through the Koala house. Koalas were predictably clinging to trees, and being comatose, but cute. Explored that path to the left and was awed at two huge, well-camouflaged wolves. They really are very shy, all curled up and faraway at the back of a pretty compound, black and gray coats all but blending into the rock.

Zoos do an awfully good job. These animals are in superb health, and an optimal setting—for a jail, that is. When and if decimation of populations occurs in the wild, through man-made or natural catastrophes such as the raging brush fires and severe drought conditions a few seasons ago in Australia—there's enough various stocks in zoos to perpetuate these whimsical creatures such as panda bears. I only hope they are storing up lots and lots of panda bear makings to protect the species against treacherous bamboo vicissitudes. I still love and remember our Olympic visitors. I was entranced by their play and their account, and would not be without one again. One can feel good about a drive and an hour's walk there and not feel obligated to stay longer than one good hour.

I was impressed by a pair of handsome mountain lions, also called Cougar, Puma, and Paint. They resemble huge house kittens but have the golden eyes of true lions, but not their heavy tawny coat. I once saw one in a canyon near Agoura. I was in my car, she was on foot. I was startled; she was stately and serene. Gave me a languorous long look and retreated with grace and dignity.

There are three classes of creature, whose existence I just cannot support: they are mosquitoes, sharks and flies. One needs vultures, let's say, for hygiene. They follow after carnivores that kill, and clean up. Sharks seem to me totally unnecessary, where stuff rots fast, doesn't smell, and enriches the sea bottom. I could live forever and ever without another shark. Ecologists, no doubt, will scream. They will say, that is where they belong, in the sea. Well, in the summer I belong in the sea too. And since I have yet to bite a shark, I think we can all readily say who is the aggressor here?

Let's be fair. I do not menace him, he menaces me.

As for mosquitoes and flies, they are dirty, breed diseases, and are plague-making. What for? Even other animals don't like them. I know about trout eating them. Big deal. We can either live without trout, or invent trout kibble. Remind me to discourse on grizzly bears next. They're the shark of the woods, and I'm all for having them rounded up onto reservations, like Indians. Ditto for alligators and crocodiles.

Summer's not too far off. Maybe I'll enlarge my thesis to include all screaming, biting, sucking creatures. Rats and mice to go, but Bunnies and capybaras can stay. Meanwhile, I'm delighted medical science has taken a big interest in sharks' hearts as well as their livers for research. Sharks are too efficient, too alien, and too monstrous for my taste. Let some survive in aquaria if they must. Bees have to stay and pollinate, but wasps can go. Aggressive critters of all phyla—into the void. Mankind is aggressor enough for me.

NEWS

News from Sunset Blvd., West of Whittier: first the bad news. Let's get it over with. Traffic is bad, all right? I don't mean slow, I mean *gridlock*. It's almost impossible to get anywhere west if the temperature on any given day is over 74 degrees Fahrenheit. Everyone wants to get to the beach. I've learned to head for the freeway even in the middle of the day, even to get to Barrington, without a grain of sand in sight. I do wish they'd stop beaming that stupid Super Bowl back East—those people snowed in back there take one look at our balmy South Seas weather, forget the smog, earthquakes and lack of housing, and decide to throw in with the rest of us struggling for a parking place in Westwood. Seriously, it's desperation time. We must not broadcast our style of living to every Hans, Tadeo and Sven who might be happy in the snow zones if only he thought it was winter everywhere, instead of just in his own *stadt*. Crowds munch at one everywhere. For instance, I rejoined Weight Watchers on Thursday, (for the billionth time, but not for about ten years. And that's another story.)

What a drastic change! There were so many people, mostly chubby women, one had to wait on line forever to get weighed, and then could hardly get close enough to the speaker to hear what she was saying. Absolutely made the situation unworkable for me-might just as well sit at home and watch an improve-yourself video.

On the other hand, there are never people when you do actually need them. Which segues nicely into the good news, about which it is high time I told you: coming west along Sunset from Beverly Hills some months ago, I noticed a boy and girl trying to scale the wall surrounding a large house on the south side of the boulevard. As my brain took a few seconds to compute this data, I realized this was a clever sculpture, as was the elderly tourists snapping a picture on the front lawn, the boy diving for his ball and the cop writing up the ticket at the curb.

What a delightful surprise-sculpture for the benefit of the passing community, not only for the generous owners cloistered inside their beautiful abode. Right out on the grass strip where anyone might see, enjoy and even steal it, for all I know. How community-minded. How astonishing in this age where toilet paper is stolen from restaurant facilities, pictures taken off hotel room walls, and a climate of fear causes some women to abandon purses and gold chains so as not to be a target for the unscrupulous young.

These playful figures remind me of the film *Poppy*, where Alan Arkin conceives the idea of a lifelike doll to fill in as a babysitter for his son. The grandmother figure is seated in a rocking chair in front of the window so all who pass by will see there is someone at home with the child. A tape playing the sound of a barking dog rounds out the notion.

People are doing a similar thing to zip onto the diamond lane of the freeway, that is, putting a life–sized doll in the passenger seat to avoid a citation, and also hostility from legit car poolers.

Pregnant women are claiming they too carry a passenger. Can't argue with that. (They never said it couldn't be internal.) I don't think they've tried to claim their cat or dog as a passenger with rights, though I may be wrong about this.

There are several huge mansions in the plush stretches of Sunset near Alta and Palm. I refer to this as the Mafia Mile—totally without factual support, incidentally—there is an air of gatedness, protection and vast money that I always think must be gangster-inspired. Anyway, one of the corner houses always has a lighted window with a foursome playing cards every single night I've ever passed it. Of course, no one walks those streets at night if they don't want to get picked up as a certifiable weirdo, so I'm moving too fast to check it out. Anyway, I prefer my fantasy that this is yet another way to protect the folks who are holed up within. Simaculums of guests or extended family spotlighted for the rubes, while the cocaine deals are cut in the basement bunker.

When you are looking for the art at 10,000 Sunset, for that is the address, be very careful that your appreciation does not result in an accident. I've seen 20 car pile-ups on the *autobahn* in Germany as people gawked at an accident. It's more dangerous than ever here in L.A.; motorists eating a croissant with one hand, steering the car with the other, and talking into a telephone cradled on their shoulder at the same time. How they do it and not kill the kids in the back seat and the dog jumping around and practically out the window… it's beyond me. I do not want a phone, a TV or a washer-dryer in the car. Not even a swimming pool. I am glad for art on my route home, but I think I'll wait for my arrival there for any stimulation greater than the news on 980 AM.

MEDITATIONS ON THE HOLIDAYS

By any other name Shakespeare said, "A rose by any other name would smell as sweet." Usually I am a big fan of the bard. None bigger. But in this particular case, I take issue with the implications. Would we inhale quite so deeply of feverthorn, I wonder? How about scarlet pollen maker? Supposing this plant was known as stinking bud or wrist-slashers or bug hider—they are full of spider, bee and aphid. And make many allergic people deathly sick.

Who says names do not influence emotions, and outcomes, for that matter? How do you think Christopher Columbus Craft ended up as director of NASA's space program? Do you not think he was a little influenced by the name, to explore where no man has gone before, in the words of Star Trek? He even includes a fast boat in his name, *Chris Craft*, that most famous of all yachts. Monikers. Been doing some thinking of the subject. Noticing that everyone in L.A. who used to be named Irving now calls himself something else. Two examples. One Irving is now *Ty*. Another is *Chip*. Both changes I can understand in light of our cultural milieux. That there is a large Thai population and Thai cooking is trendy, modestly priced and generally delicious. There is also something sporty, and breezily gentile about this name, Ty Cobb…it could smack of country-clubs and college guys out riding around in a convertible. Voila: good vibes. Same is true for *Chip*. Subliminally speaking, chips evoke chocolate. Poker. Computer. Cow. Here too, the subconscious associations are now to stuff, new stuff, future stuff. How can tired, back east old Irving compare to this kind of clout? Irving has to do with relatives, boiled chicken, and Bayonne, New Jersey. See what I mean? Just like San Francisco has ruined Bruce for all time, so have other times, other sensibilities ruined Gertrude, Agnes, Clarence. Hector. Even a Trojan Achilles can become illogically obsolete. Although I'm taken with the Heathers, Devons and Brittanies, all in all it might be safer to stick to classic names that do not come in and out of fashion, but are always-while not *wow*—are not *thud*, either. Such as Cynthia. Grace. Elizabeth. John. Michael. Alexander. I have never known a Nancy or Diana I did not like and admire. To me, they are the sunniest, happiest names, and their bearers are too. How do you think you might react to being fixed up on a blind date with an Elmer, Elroy, Egbert or Sisal? See? You're going to know a very great deal about the family, region and socioeconomic level of this person even before you lay eyes on him, and if he's a hunk, I'll be surprised. Most probably, he's a tractor salesman from Sears. Or teaches Sunday School at the Baptist church. He is the male counterpart of Mildred, Doris and Beulah, the orthopedic loafer set.

Be wary of the heavily regional. Parents who name infants Jo-Bob, Sue-Ann, Willoughby and Ruthi-Mae might be resented once the kid from Mobile wants to go into stock-brokering in Manhattan. Best to give what I call a Ralph Lauren type name. Well-worn, but elegant. American neutral. Stay away from ethnic if you want to move into the mainstream. Ebenezer, Obadiah and Morris have been laugh cues for too many sitcoms to go down well. Just as it's as well not to settle down in Azusa, Cucamonga or Yakima, Washington. If at all possible.

And what of my son's new dentist, Dr. Moan? I know another named Pain. What profession do you think Dr. Whizzwell practices? If you said urology, you're right.

Parents can, and do, express quite a bit of sadism, as well as originality in their bestowal of names on their helpless infants. Some cultures rejoice in originality. Ima and Youra Hogg, daughters of a Texas psychiatrist, do seem to be beyond the pale of parental license. There was a recent study report of prison inmate names that is suggestive. Lethal, Oder and Vere were four times more frequent than other names. Lethal?

In my salad days, I knew some cute Slugs, Skips and Slammers. Now maybe the girls go for a Sting, a Pink Floyd or a Killer, I don't know. Seems like the more bizarre the name, the better, especially if you go for heavy metal. On a personal note, I was considered a trend-setter, far-out or crazy, depending on one's point of view in '58 when I named my first born Joshua. My parents begged me to reconsider this weird idea. He was the only Josh in our neighborhood, or any of the schools he ever attended at that time. Now he complains that every other little tot he knows is named Josh. Can I help it if I am prescient?

There are numerous names in every walk of life that have predicted the outcome of the bearer. What happens if John Greenleaf Longfellow doesn't want to become a poet? He is in big trouble. Likewise, does Satan Goldberg have to become the anti-Christ? So watch the programming you do before you fill out that baptism form. Check in with your local minister, or friendly therapist. Before the poor kid has to take up the cudgels and fight for his life in the schoolyard, or become a book burner. Just because there are prominent exceptions, like the Zappas...Dweezil, Moon, Lala, Ahmet and Diva…don't be fooled. Most people not in the rock or Hollywood biz don't survive.

THURSDAY, DECEMBER 21—OR FRIDAY—OR SOMETHING

This is as tropical as it ever gets, my dears. The little bure in which we are housed has mundane bathroom cabinets, small white-tiled shower walls and floor, beside dressers that could be found in every other house in the valley. But not all over—not so. Big, stout mahogany trunks are embedded in the corners of the house—seemingly to help hold them up. More branches hold up the ceiling—these are rougher, with bud stalks, curves and knots all over. Beautiful woven straw rugs cover the floors—vivid, fragrant, unreal-looking blossoms adorn every surface.

The faces, and the really strange language the natives speak to each other when they are not speaking their grade school English, illustrates that we are very far indeed from the oo-oo ah-ah uh-uh of the Hawaiian language. Even the names of our house-couple are strange—Saforosa and Onissino.

After dinner, Hubby started asking how they said hello, goodbye, please, thank you in Fijian—a few basic phrases. Now, I hate to make him out to be light in the loafers—or to start a collection of Hubby jokes like Phyllis Diller and her husband Fang—but Hubby started right into one of his two worst things.

Neither he nor I are talented at languages—I, however, keep quiet about it. Not he. Wherever he is, he seeks to learn a little of the native tongue to make new friends and be simpatico. Unfortunately, since he has a terrible ear for it, it often ends up the opposite way!

These simple phrases are amazingly complicated to say—very, very odd, their language. Also, each island has its own variant—very different from the other. The language sounds like it could be Indonesian, New Guinean, Bornean—like some of the faces of the people. Hubby tried valiantly for half an hour to repeat a few phrases.

"Rosa" patiently corrects him every time—sometimes quietly informing us his version is a swear word.

Hubby contorts his face, cheeks and mouth valiantly struggling with the vowels.

I am working on their two names, plus how to pronounce the name of the Island, which although spelled Laucaula, is pronounced *Lau thala.* We're sitting in the beach gazebo, South Pacific style, waiting for breakfast while gazing out at a languid sea on which many brown coconuts are bobbing like so many shrunken heads.

Oh yes, Hubby's number two thing he's not so good at—besides language—is hitting a tropical resort and being able to tell when he's had enough sun.

We are using large amounts of coconut oil on his poor back and sides—the parts he exposes when he snorkels face down for hours searching for shells.

He is medium-rare. Looks like a slab of filet mignon, au naturelle. Any more sun today and we will be exploring the exotic nearby hospital. Stranger and stranger—he does it every time.

I think when we go native, a sort of Zelig effect takes over and he refuses to admit being a pink-skinned gringo. He wants to be Che Guevara. He wants to be Shaquille O'Neil. He wants to be Paul Roberson. He wants to be Othello.

In Hawaii and Mexico, where this routinely happens, the natives rush out to cut and lay on the aloe.

In Laucaula, we are in the midst of a working copra plantation, so of course, here Saforosa runs for the coconut oil.

In Spain, we got olive oil!

I think it's the softening, soothing emollient texture that eases and moistens the tortured skin.

Today, I will police him—he cannot be trusted!

(When am I going to get to my term paper on Dora, Hans and the Rat Man: Freud's Greatest Hits or Loony Tunes. Wouldn't they make a good rock group? Better than Pink Floyd or the Bitches.)

I think I write to avoid writing my thesis.

I'm idly speculating about how people write fiction. Maybe you think up a character first. What to name him or her? The only name I can come up with is Lithia. Will she do and think all the things I do? Should I change my name to protect my parents and children?

SUNDAYS AND HOLIDAYS

I just hate it when Sundays and Holidays come right in a row, like they did this year. Both Christmas and New Years fell on a Sunday; the next day was the official holiday. There is never enough forethought or planning to make it through these bleak times without some sort of severe deprivation or trauma, I don't care how much time it takes to get ready for it. Owning six or seven calendars, I was aware that this was going to happen to me. One weekend we were out of town, the other we were home. Out of town was better; we all stayed well, I had my electric blanket and warm up suit with me, I avoided terminal hypothermia in San Francisco, although I never did get into my silk dress for Christmas. I put it on for three minutes, almost died of the cold and got right back into my sweats...make that clean sweats for Christmas Day.

New Year's weekend was different. We were all home, and Hubby came down with stomach flu. I had actually anticipated that others might catch it, so we stocked up on Kaopectate at the pharmacy against what might be a long, shitty weekend. Three bottles proved to be too little. Ditto, two bottles of Tylenol. No take-out restaurants were open to spare me in the kitchen. I've heard of old airplanes and metal fatigue, but I never had heard of silicon fatigue; our thermometer developed it and splintered. So did all the returning offspring. There was not a whole, healthy person in the lot—everyone looked like a refuge from Bhopal, it was a crisis... There was not enough Pepto-Bismol to make a dent in the distress, or even somewhat offset sore tummies, and *not* a danged one of my usual delivery places would so much as answer their phone.

What a mess, we were locked out of our normal supply lines for two whole days. I felt like Admiral Byrd at the South Pole. All doctors were away, all their offices shut. Not only Christians, but Buddhists and Jewish people pack it up and go skiing or to Cancun or somewhere over Christmas, and one is left feeling like Fred Astaire in *On the Beach*...one of the last persons alive anywhere, forever.

All holiday parties went on without us. We could have been on the moon. We ran out of tangerines, vitamin C, apple juice and bananas. We had enough rice and spaghetti. Oh well, so we would be a fat family with rickets.

I want to go on record: One day to celebrate is more than enough. Two days of the whole world being closed down is one day too many for me. I might need to go shopping, or buy a new hat. Certainly there are a lot of presents at that time, but they are what someone else imagines I need, not what I may actually need. I'm not used to a world shut down; I may not go there, but I want to have a place to go to in case I want to. I want options!

Anyone else get withdrawal-from-the-world pangs at Christmas?

SPRAY, OR BOOGIEING UP TO BAKERSFIELD

Who the heck says that Southern California is just a big wasteland, that there's no beauty left here? Hey, there's a lot of lovely stuff, if you just know what to look for and where and when to find it. It's incredible what you won't see in L.A.'s close environs—because of the smog, because there's little reason to look up at night—but it's there for the asking throughout the rest of Southern California.

Not long ago, I had a choice, an unusual night-time opportunity to go beyond L.A. First, of course, I'd allowed myself to get out of my familiar west side rut. After seeing my last psychoanalytic patient of the day, I went to my Panasonic to pick up my phone messages. There was an excited one from my trial lawyer Hubby, then battling baddies in Bakersfield Superior Court.

I thought I had definitely missed the chance to hear him in his upcoming closing argument, but no. He told me "Come quick, I'm closing my arguments tomorrow, Thursday morning." He knew I might be able to re-arrange my schedule for Thursday mornings.

Shuffling patients around isn't something I like to do, but I felt it was important to be there to listen to Hubby's case, which resembled an Old Testament saga. So I told him yes, I would make it—I would take a last-minute two-hour excursion to Bakersfield on Wednesday night.

Wednesday at dinnertime, I threw a heat-resistant bowl of soup into the microwave, zapped its contents to lukewarm and guzzled them down. Then I packed my nightie and my dental care equipment (more than a toothbrush, but less than the heavy artillery and material that General Patton packed for the Battle of the Bulge), rounded up my portable CD player with its little auto lighter power cord, and off I went! I would climb the mountain passes to wafting classical music.

And what a perfect, balmy January night in which to do so. Even at 7:30 pm, it was perfect for sliding back the sunroof. I say, what a life! With the roof half-open, I'd soon cleared the haze of the northern valley. I noticed that a huge full moon hovered above me. The night sky, dark blue over the Santa Clarita Valley—why, I felt plunged into the surreal surroundings of Rousseau's African Sleeping Gypsy.

The full moon made the mountaintops look snowy, changing the serene brown landscape into something improbably, exotically Alpine. Taking the twists and turns, swoops and banks of the bright white mountains reminded me of driving the *Autobahn* through Berteschgaden.

I'd just never seen this stretch of I-5 as poetically charming as on this winter night. I never saw it so clear, like black crystal. Driving at night was so much less mundane, so much more alluring and mysterious, than driving in the daytime in the Hughes-Castaic Lake area.

And then I realized my cruise control wasn't working. That is, I found I was doing a lot more accelerator pushing uphill that I thought would be necessary. It was uncomfortable. So I pulled off the road into a Texaco station, hoping to get the fuse or wire or whatever was responsible quickly fixed.

The attendant was really helpful. He squinted around the dash and under it, but, alas, he couldn't find anything, as he hailed from Baltimore.

Hubby and I just jawed with a lot of those guys in Sanibel—their accent is a lot like that of nearby Williamsport, Pennsylvania, my hometown. A musician, he was tickled and amazed I'd pegged his city of origin. He promised to send me a tape of his songs and performances. I gave him my card.

Onward, pedal not quite to the metal, working enough that my hip muscles were soon tired. It almost felt like my foot was surgically attached to the floorboard. And, before I knew it, I was going much faster than I'd ever driven at night. And I thought, why not? No one around, seemingly no CHP's certainly, just some pokey truckers.

A gestalt hit me: were anything else to fail, I could be a trucker, one with a faulty cruise control. For horn solos, I'd play my CD-player through an amplifier. I say, what a life! Hey, I'm a night nymph by nature anyway. I wouldn't mind the trucking profession, except perhaps for truck stop food. Well, then, I'd pack my own lunch.

God, I thought, this air is so drastically different from that of West L.A. So pristine was it up Frazier Park, Thomas Mann could have built, staffed and written about the sanitorium right here in Southern California. It was only once I got to the other side of the grapevine, the descent that the tule fog rolled in, blotting out some of the magic. Suddenly it was a dull, drab Wednesday night in the weed patch, the pumpkin patch known as Arvin. But it was still exciting. Turnoffs beckoned the Mojave Edwards Air Force Base, Palmdale. I've been to those places, of course, but the air was so damned gorgeous tonight, I was tempted to venture as far afield as possible. I recalled in time that my destination was Bakersfield. I proceeded without further ado.

The trip proved that there are still a few, undeveloped, poppy strewn patches of real California between the valley and the altar-sprayed melons of Kern County. I don't think they've decided to spray anything there yet. To the East is Santa Paula, where the Burpee Company may conceivably be flying low over the roses, but with genetically modified bumblebees, not aircraft and poison.

CROWD AT MING LAKE OUTSIDE BAKERSFIELD.

Ming Lake after dark; and a rough lot they are too. It is like *Marjorie Morningstar*, dewy innocence and the American dream waking up next to *Mad Max* or the *Clockwork Orange* protagonist. A future full of young people too disillusioned to do anything but spoil it for others. The spoilers—beat yourself up and everything else around you in your despair. Mexicans particularly seem to optimize this split. Most are eagerly working to make it up to the middle class—to Penny's and Sear's, to the PTA and Halloween Eve. Others furiously reject and despoil their surroundings in society, vandalize the schools—do they feel the pain and wounding of a deficit background? The most savage and assaultive of their gangs that prey particularly on school neighborhoods in parts of Los Angeles call themselves The Crips—short for Cripples? That sort of says it all, doesn't it? They feel crippled by their beginnings; they can't stand the feelings of inferiority, of helplessness, in this the more affluent new America, so they set out to blow it all away. The world in microcosm in Kern County, the human condition—not so terribly pretty at times.

Even psychoanalysis, what I am currently reading, says these same depressing things—that even sweet chubby-cheeked little nurslings cuddling up to the breast may have these same savage instincts. What?! I invariably protest, this tender little pink butterball, this downy fuzzy baby chick? Yep, says Melanie Klein, this adorable infant is enraged that the breast it needs for milk, warmth and skin contact, in short, the very items that represent everything good that the baby must have to survive, it also hates and wishes destroyed. Why? Why? Why? Because the breast goes away, it is not always on tap, it may not respond when the baby screams in desperate hunger as fast as it is needed. Therefore, since it is not completely under the baby's control or attached to the baby like its toes and fingers, the baby considers it to be part and parcel of its body and its much valued self. But it isn't; it has a mind of its own and goes away when it wants to. The baby doesn't like this behavior at all. So, you see, the dilemma—entitlement, possession, rage at the loss of the good smells, tastes and feels of the skin, primal rage, impotence; get it? Gangs, wars, Cain, Abel, Raskolnikov, *Crime and Punishment*, literature, art and death – all this good stuff and it starts with a baby and the breast. Some days it all seems pretty sad and futile.

Rage and anger built into the cutest packages. Adorable when full, clean, and rested, angry monsters the rest of the time?

SCENES-EN-MISE

It's a consolation, really, when at last it starts to pour. I have, after all, been carrying my scarf and umbrella and wearing my raincoat every day. Britain is an island and I well remember Hawaii, where the motto is: "If you don't like the weather, be patient, it will change in about 15 minutes."

One great delight when my brolly does get a workout is that I see one of my favorite sights—London babies being prammed along, totally shielded from the driving, drizzling, or dumping rainstorm by plastic bonnet-to-bootie pram covers.

I think I love to see these kids' little forms, so quiet under their Lucite, because of the sheer inventiveness of this protective membrane and because their still, withdrawn forms so remind me of the work we did last autumn with newborns. They were similarly withdrawn and protected in their post-partum womb-like Lucite shells, their half-way stations on the way to sentient personhood.

I've never seen a British infant squalling under his woolies and plastic amniotic environment. It must feel familiar, a solid membrane removed from the *sturm und drang* of the violent elements out there—from the rush of circulating fluids, water and blood, so necessary to its growth. But noisy.

TV FOOD

There are restrictions against showing addictive, harmful substances on TV shows. You cannot have ads showing people quaffing their favorite lite brews. Nor can you have ads showing folks snorting, sniffing or sticking themselves with narcotic substances designed to walk them into nirvana-like states imbibing material until a trance state is reached. I want parity of substance abuse!

It is not fair that some harmful agents are banned, and not others. As I recover from my osseous surgery on my gums, I ponder this unfairness.

It seems some may have shown, no really, may have pushed hard with the goal of selling, selling, selling these items to addicted unfortunates. They luxuriously gratify their appetites with life-threatening stuffs, with the greatest impunity.

Who are these malefactors, and how did it happen?

They are the purveyors of Dove Bars, Frito-Lay's Almond Mounds Bars, McDonald's wares and teensy Ritz Crackettes, tobogganing down peanut butter slopes. All filled with cholesterol, saturated fats, calories, and enough lipids to give me two strokes and a by-pass.

For thirteen days now, I have been finding myself singing "Give me a break, *give me a break,* give me one of those Kit-Kat bars." "Just for the fun of it, Diet Coke." The new Elton John, Paula Abdul commercial which I saw on the music awards special just sizzles, and was the best thing on that program where one is mandatorily sent away when addicted enough, that doesn't mean we are not as threatened as the problem cocaine abuser. They wouldn't think of touting coke on the major networks. I'd like the same consideration. Even smoking is being banned on all airlines, where do I go to avoid airplane food, a hard sell for vanilla and chocolate products, and ruffle ridge potato chips?

Pray tell, who will admit that unnecessary foods are ruining our blood fats and waistlines? People in this country are either starving to death in shelters for the homeless, or dropping dead of heart attacks from too much propaganda on TV Shows. Those of us with no will power would have channels that glorify only carrots, grapefruits and bean sprouts. I think it is unfair to show cheddar stuffed potatoes, milkshakes and doughnuts to those of us with cholesterol levels more than 2054. Is there a decent network who would like to be the first to abstain? After all, they said it couldn't be done. Folks wouldn't stand for it, they needed their fix. Ten years later, if they need their fix, tough luck, let them do without in favor of the good majority. If they feel that way about junk food.

Even one of my favorites, Jay Leno, is now pushing greasy corn chips on prime time. Disgusting. Anything they have to pay thousands of dollars a second to sell, you can be sure is not good for you. The good stuff is so cheap, no one can afford to advertise on TV. Only if it's not moving well, and you don't need it anyways, do they hire someone gorgeous to peddle it. Eggs have gotten a bad rap, sure they're using Peter Graves to snake-out charm eggs into your bloodstream. When's the last time you heard a P.R man selling for asparagus, broccoli or celery?

I'll tell you when, only when they re-embed it in some gooey goop that ups the price and calorie count, and is packaged to a fare thee well by a food processor who takes out the good, and coats, fries, bakes or breads into the bar. Sure, I'm a sorehead. But I am on this damned New Year's diet, I've lost six pounds but it's precarious. I've resorted to Channel 28 to escape the heavy food ads. Right now, I'm watching Indian dances and they're good, but sooner or later, I'm going to want some plot. There's only so much enlightenment I can stand in one weekend, I've mastered *the quark. friend or foe,* for today.

And would like to segue into some nice, non-threatening sitcom that won't threaten my sobriety. But I fear running into an ad for Valentine's Day candies, coming up next weekend, to Coca-Cola, by far the best ads running. They always make me want a Classic.

What's a poor couch potato, minus the fat-loading, to do? I know, try the video store. Forget it; the last one advised me to stock up on Good & Plenty and settle down to the show. As it happened, I did. They are now my all time favorites. KCET, do your stuff and may Bill Moyers retain his Nielsen ratings, and let the calories fall where they may.

EMPTY CALORIES

I have never supposed that losing weight was easy. In this culture, we are surrounded by overt and covert messages pushing food of every sort, so that even on a strong abstemious day, I am tempted by succulent fair in unlikely places; that is, I flee the high-calorie kitchen, only to be assaulted by Michael Jackson writhing around frosty mugs of Real Coke or Lynn Redgrave stripping her cape off in front me, some linguini marinara and 10,000 salivating weight watchers. It has never been a snap to say no to potato chips, pork rinds and pot roast, especially when they are flashed onto the TV screen in subliminal jolts, so that a person can hardly get her defenses up and ready.

For the last months I have been, well not as good as gold, but somewhat sterling about modifying my bad eating habits and "making better choices" as my nutritional counselor puts it. Maybe I have been 70/30 *on* my diet, but I have lost a little, concentrating heavily on victuals for the bovine, i.e., greens, sprouts, and herbage of all degrees of crinkle, curl and country of origin (endive, mache from Brazil; that sort of thing). It's been a bit of a trial and I only hope my back teeth hold out. They've gotten a fearsome workout for someone who is not three-toed, with four stomachs and wallowing in mud.

But now, for the unkindest cut of all. My sources tell me, and my sources are *The New York Times* and *The National Enquirer*...junk reading...That food ain't what it used to be! The very same pasturage folks munched down in the Paleolithic days now has very different nourishing qualities. In other words, I could chaw that stuff all night and be getting the proper qualities out of it.

Yes fellow sufferers, the bitter greens we gag down in the hope of transforming ourselves into Audrey Hepburns are, according to S. Boyd Easton in his tome, *The Paleolithic Prescription,* much less nutritious than the original wild plant foods eaten by our early forbears. Thousands of years of plant breeding and modern food processing have greatly increased simple, less desirable sugars, decreased many needed carbohydrates and increased calorie content. Their food was 4.13% higher in protein and 12.6% higher in fiber.

Their meats averaged only 4.3 % fats, as compared to 25 to 35 % in supermarket meats, what fat there was, was less saturated because of diet.

The moral of this story is: *no wonder it's such a battle. Even if you adhere religiously to your bunny-rabbit/grasshopper regime.*

"*The moment you quit loping across the veldt like Cornell Wilde and slow down for a nosh at Peppone's, the old love handles are going to re-appear.*"

I was there for lunch; I had an abstemious bowl of Sicilian calamari. Even the tomato sauce and olive oil, as compared with butter and garlic, didn't prevent a split at the back seam of my pants as I exited. Any departure from the inhuman, non-food offered by Nutrisystem put bulges where lines had been. I have been semi-Nutrisysteming it...their food is so freeze-dried and processed, I doubt if there's an erg of food value left in it. You get to supplement their foiled follies with fresh salads and yogurts; those are, I suspect, along with the vitamin pills, what keep you going. I'm sure thiamine and citric acids are back at the plant in Pennsylvania. If you eat their stuff, and only their stuff, you may get thin. But you don't feel happy.

The happy authors of *The Prehistoric Diet* say that it is programmed into us to gorge on salt, sweet and fats when these commodities are available. Because they are *such* a rarity in the wild. The body rules the mouth; but the mind can rule our body.

Even with the most stringent behavior, eating the right things will not put us in the great shape our ancestors were in.

We'd have to forswear civilization and go squat in the scrub with some aborigines who have not bothered with new and improved plant life, but have respected and left the original alone. They know about the preservation and have established a benign balance with their environment. If only we were as sensible enough to take a trip to Ayers Rock, as an alternative to more months on Nutrisystem, it sounds very attractive. I'll lope with the antelope, wail with some wallaby, and join them in recreating their "Dreamtime." My dreamtime would be of endless natural food having the right proportion of fats and calories, so I could fit into size sevens. I'd happily settle for a size-small sarong, the hell with Chanel. Who needs her in the outback anyway? There has got to be an answer to yo-yo dieting, and I may just have found it. It'll be hard on the spouse and kiddies, but they can pack up their bowie knives and come too, if they won't miss the tube too much. Wonder if *The New York Times* gets delivered to Alice Springs?

DIET

The Brits are slender and upright. The Brits are self-contained. But... the Brits never stop eating.

They eat hearty porridge breakfasts, hearty meat-pie luncheons, teas with three kinds of crust-less sandwiches, usually sardine, salmon and cucumber on buttered bread, then a strawberry tart and a meringue with flavored whipped cream. Later, of course, supper. Meat or fish and four kinds of veggies—courgettes (zucchini), often among them.

Now I ask you—how come they are slender and athletic looking? Genetics is your answer.

An Italian, Greek or Slav would balloon up on all this. Not your Celt. Don't give me the cold—it's been very mild. Oh—add vast amounts of cream and butter to everything of course!

They also seem to walk very briskly, I might add. Also do lots of bird-watching and general rustling about in the shrubbery, burning off lots of calories in the country, I suppose, and climbing steps—thousands of them; in the Underground.

London is an up-and-down city, all right. In L.A., we spread out and drive. Here, up and down. The theaters—we climbed up for 20 minutes to see *Cats*—and that was inside the theater!

OVEREATERS ANONYMOUS

What have I to do with them hard-breathing, heavy-hipped humans hunting about grimly in the half-lit meeting room of the First Baptist Church, half-lit themselves with the local ecstasy? Of placing themselves in the Divine Hands of the Great Goodies Dispenser?

Of admitting, yes, wallowing in the fact of being unregenerate, compulsive over eaters?

Others stuff themselves with other types of leaves and grains.

The hope of casting off loathsomeness makes their blubber fairly bubble! Ugh, let me escape into the coolness of the night from these flunking fools and grant, Celestial Skinniness, that I may never meet a mirror.

SMOKE

It's come to me with a bang that I am having irreconcilable differences with a classmate of mine, who is a heavily addicted smoker. We simply cannot have dinner together anymore, which is a real loss. She patronizes only restaurants where she can leisurely enjoy her cigarettes; I go only to smokeless environments. I used to accompany her to the smoking section on occasion; her insistence on being able to do so was so complete I hoped I could tough it out.

We've had conversations about it in which she laughs and says it is probably an identification with her father, whom she adores and enjoys. Another friend who does not smoke is tolerant toward it because of her father's smoke, and the familiar and loving atmosphere it recreates for her.

We just saw *Accused*, the new Kelly McGillis and Jody Foster film, in which Jody is gang raped on a pin ball machine in a bar. That's when this conviction that smoke is a form of rape hit me. During my entire childhood, my father chain-smoked cigars. Now this was back in the thirties and forties; smokers' lib was non-existent and children's lib even less so. His smoke infiltrated every cell of my existence when he was home, and was part of my life when he was not. When I sat on the cushions of the chintz clean towel from the linen closet, and we were expected to use it for one week...it was already impregnated with cigar smoke smell, don't ask me how; I guess this form of tobacco is, or was when they came from Cuba, notoriously pungent.

I received absolutely no back-up from anyone for the idea that these conditions were obnoxious; quite the contrary. It was more like "how dare you complain about your father," in fact, I didn't; since I vastly preferred him, cigar and all, to others in the family. Mother didn't smoke, but she did fume, splutter and vituperate like an old, cranky engine. I also didn't know what manic-depressive meant in those days, but she was one, and had the temper to match, irritable and explosive. I liked my father, so why didn't I like his cigar, his familiar, his Pywacket? By all the principles of global generalization from that which you like to accoutrements, why did I not take to ole Smellos like Pop? He was just as allergic as I am; as is my classmate. I guess they just make an exception for their favorite substance. My friend teaches me the meaning of addiction. Not only does she have active asthma and allergies to animals, needing to use inhalers and allergy medications but she owns cats, dogs, and horses. She has even written a doctoral thesis explaining what the use of tobacco means to her, that it is a means to keep from disappearing psychologically, and believes all this with all her heart, going so far as to say that she will quit when her doctor says she should. I guess when a patient comes in and says everyone says I should quit, and I need someone who won't tell me that, are you that person? Someone will say yes, rents being what they are in Beverly Hills. Meanwhile, the admired father is down with congestive heart failure. Emphysema and cancer of the kidney. My classmate is still smoking. I called her tonight after *Accused* to say that if we are to meet for dinner before class, it will have to be in the non-smoking section, or not at all. (First time I've put my foot down, so powerful is the force of her conviction/addiction that she has the right. Which of course, she does.) She said, "Sorry, I can't smoke all day. I'm in session with people, so..." So…she needs that time for smoking. The smoking initiative has done well, taxing and cigarettes and I have been taught by Jody Foster not to be a victim anymore, by God, I'm standing up for myself. It was her irritability that always made me back down before, and her absolute belief in the rightness of her position. For now, we can co-exist only in class, where no smoking is allowed. The damned smoke is so invasive, so absolutely aggressive; it is very much like rape to the mucous linings of eyes, nose, throat, and lungs to me. I remember clearly sitting in beauty parlors and at lunch counters dying of smoke, when my request for the next person to please not smoke at me would be greeted be a hateful, almost violent answer...If you don't like it lady, you can get out of here. Who says there isn't any good progress? Of course, the air and water had to get a whole lot worse before the environmentalists took any action, but, it's happening now. We are not liable to breathe the air in L.A., but there is not the fatuous denial; the problem is grave, we are aware of this.

My friend is living in denial. For cigarette smokers, there is a no A.A. She functions fine at her job. So powerful is her denial that smoking is hurting her, or can hurt her, she has her husband defending her smoking even though he has quit himself, and only lights up now when she is attacked for smoking even though others in the group have asked her not to. The fact that they are both highly intelligent folks in the field of psychoanalysis, with doctorates in psychology, matters not a whit; we humans have an almost endless capacity to deceive ourselves, it was just much more difficult with friends. I always ended up feeling so mean for depriving someone of what they needed so badly.

But now I am a hard-core non-smoker, no exceptions. I almost died last year on a flight to Fiji when they ran out of non-smoking seating, forcing me to breathe smoke for many hours; I had a serious setback in my recovery from pneumonia as a result, and my whole trip was spoiled by illness.

Denial is a fascinating mechanism; it really means *everyone but me. Sure, this is true for every one but me.* I've got a few, seat belts, overweight, sometimes my teeth don't get their evening brushing, I just rinse a little Plax around. But I've never raped anyone else with my plaque, at least I hope not, and a whiplash will hurt only my own neck. My extra avoirdupois does not deposit fatty deposits in anyone else's arteries. But when "Sue" abuses a substance, we all abuse that substance. We proved on this fall's referendum that no matter how much the tobacco industry spends, it still cannot convince us that it's anti-American not to like side steam smoke blown in one's face, that tobacco smokers have the right to life, liberty, and bad lungs for everyone. Why, that stuff is worse than a houseful of radon gas.

REGRESSION?

They are keeping something from us. Scientists have never, to my knowledge, written about vestigial scent–making glands behind the ears of human beings. Oh, medical experts pay plenty of attention to ears proper, inner ears, ear drums, ear diseases. Ear tube operations are highly contested and common events requiring major anesthesia. But nary a word about that neglected kingdom of Behind The Bar. I watch *Wild Animal Kingdom* regularly, and they regularly show beasts marking their territory; they rub, spray or paw the scent our of glands ranging from under the eye, in the African Dik-Dik, to those many other critters who store their portable surveyors' accessories in a gland under their tails, or-so odd!-on their wrist, as do the rare ring-tailed Madagascar kinkajous.

The secretion from these glands is specialized for marking property and domain; it is not for courtship, mating or rearing their young, so far as we know. Other rituals, behaviors and colorations serve to achieve those life-functions.

This material has texture and enough body to linger on wood, grass or even bare earth, for substantial periods of time. Some great animals, like the tiger, need huge amount of space for hunting and the security of the feeling at ease…though they spray replenish their boundaries frequently, the scent must stick to the jungle…for a sizable of time.

Hence my conviction that I can't really speak for anyone else with total candor. I have an area behind my ears that emits a sticky, waxy substance with a distinct, in fact *very* distinct, shall we say, perfume. I mean, you could just say it smelt bad, but would it to some other species?...we don't know. What else could its message possibly be?

Anyway, no matter how carefully I wash there each day, the scent returns almost immediately. My otolaryngologist, who periodically removes the wax from inside my ears, says there is absolutely no such thing as scent marker in humans, and that I certainly do not have any such thing.

What does he know! Now, I'm not one of these crazies who think they smell bad when they don't. Psychiatric literature is full of those folks with thought and perceptual disorders. I don't even have smelly feet and am remarkably dry and of neutral fragrance under my arms. Oh, I rinse with Plax and brush my teeth like everyone else, and emit strong odors after garlic and onions; but in general, though I love being freshly bathed and shampooed, and don't think I smell any worse than others do, probably better, *except behind the ears*, than the great unwashed masses, wherever they still may be, in Calcutta or shelters for the homeless. Certainly those of us on the west side are over-washed with too much soap and too hot water, according to dermatologists. And granted, Madison Avenue has stampeded most of us into almost phobic anxiety about whether or not we smell. And granted, the backs of one's ear are an area very, very few persons have any access to: nevertheless, I use a little swab to remove the material and smell for myself. And yep, it's there. There is *no* other single spot in or on my carcass that has an odor that is not connected, and firmly connected, to a clear, well understood biological function.

Is this not interesting and overlooked data that might present some fascinating links with other species? Could I be a throwback to some other genus? No, don't tell me it is oil from my hair that runs down behind my ear…I don't believe that. I can have a secretion when my hair is newly washed, with no oils whatsoever, or only good-smelling ones.

Anyone wants to fund me grant money to go to the zoo armed with a carton of Q-Tips and do the necessary field work? Or should I just lend my ears to the Oregon Mammal Research Institute?

THE NOSE KNOWS

It's been a rough winter, flu and upper respiratory-tract-wise, but there's been an odd up-side for me.

I've turned into a regular "nose". You know what I mean by a nose, do you? I don't mean a person who *has* a nose, I mean a person who *is* a nose! That is, one whose extraordinary sense can discern smells, essences and qualities of foods, coffees or perfumes many times more sensitively than others. A valuable talent, worth big bucks in the marketplace.

Dogs and cats may not enter this contest; we all know the four-footed can easily leave us mere two-foots in the dust, olfactory-wise. We are not even contenders (as in "I could've been a contender") with the rest of the planet's fauna. When it comes to smell, we rank in a disabled, or very dense, per centile. Is there a word that describes non, or minimally, smelling? If so, I don't know it...what is that analogous adjective or adverb, in the kingdom of the schnoz, to deaf, mute, blind or dumb?

Ordinary mortals can get the high notes and the low notes, as those in the perfume trade say, and an occasional off note. But the knowledge of what is great or simply okay is what makes or breaks the eight-figure sniffer. In other words, the lowly proboscis, brunt of joke (and racial prejudice) over the eons, may truly be more the seat of the soul than we dreamed. Certainly it can be the instrument, along with vision, for discerning the heavenly.

Divine *parfums* rely on sometimes less than divine ingredients. Oh yes, there are attars of lilacs and roses, gardenia and frangipani, but it only becomes perfume when balanced out with ambergris from whales, musk from scent glands and other lowly animal materials. The heady florals must mix with more earthly products to give the substance the ability to cling and last, otherwise it would be like wafting a lovely bloom through the room...yes...delicious, but too evanescent to shell out $90 bucks an ounce.

Even the palate relies very heavily on the nose, have you noticed when you're all stuffed up your taste buds are still there, but without cooperation from a working sense of smell, they do their job badly at best? (This is a valley-girl sentence…a lot of inflection at the end?)

I've hunted always for a certain scent, lily of the valley. I have loved those fragrant little blooms above all others, when they first make their way out of the furled green leaves in the early spring. They remind me of the garden in my childhood home of Williamsport, PA, there was a self-renewing patch in the stones near the back wall, and every April, like magic, they would proffer their little serrated white bells to the noses of passing bees and to me.

The lily of the valley scents I have since tried, "*muguet des bois*" in French, lilies of the wood, have not quite had the right magic smell, my nose was titillated, both domestic and foreign lily scents, just missed. It had something to do with creating a delicious lack of boundary, or connection, between me and another time and place. Some essences seemed to be terrific; the first few moments were wonderful. Then something went flat.

What the madeleine was to Proust's taste buds, the lily is to my non-verbal olfactory receptors, the magic gate to the world of my childhood. Those lost childhood memories still eluded me.

But the *nose* has its ways. Recently, it's been acting up something terrible, with sinus, and viral clogups, a veritable gridlock of the snout. This necessitated a call, an urgent call in to my allergist-I'm positively addicted to breathing…silly me. He tried a few different solutions, all of them, seemingly, needing to be sprayed right into the nostrils.

One was sea water bought at the pharmacy and called *ocean*; another—some stinging cortisone nose drop, and last, a miraculous fluid to be sprayed in, dear readers, exactly like the lilies of the valley that grew at the bottom of my childhood garden, adjacent to the alley and Mr. Moore's property line. Smells like the big Easter lilies as well. Poetic justice…the perfect scent arising out of an allergic condition. I am to infuse this delectable substance into my nostrils twice a day, perhaps indefinitely. Doctor's orders. It smells perfect, no bad after tones, and no low tones at all. Though it doesn't last too long, you get to renew it frequently, and right at the target area, not wasting it behind knees or ears, but right on, or in, what would be the G-spots to sex, the S-for-smell-spots!

No more am I wakened by the deep rich bubble of Folgers to look forward to; no, I head for the good old drug of my choice to my pillow at night, thankful to be breathing in, or breathing at all, actually, the heady aroma of bechlomethasone dipropianate, monohydrate, microcrystalline cellulose, carboxymethylellulse sodium, dextrose, benzalkonium, choride, polysorbate 80, and 0.25% v/w phenylethy alcohol. Ah, nature…ain't it grand?

I knew there was something good about the flu epidemic this winter…it's an ill wind that blows no one any good. Or should I say blows *no nose* some good?

MODERN HAZARDS

I often think of myself as sort of an upscale Erma Bombeck. Mostly, I love Erma's column and can identify her stories of family *sturm und drang* with my own family of about ten years ago. I've moved onward and upward into a higher level of consternations and perplexities since then: from pimples-and-socks-eaten-up-by-the-washing-machine type of troubles to those of a higher order of sophistication. With my children in their twenties instead of their teens, our family has moved from how-to-pay-for-braces-and-summer-camps to how-to-pay-for-trips-to-Nepal-and their psychoanalyses.

I used to just scribble in my notebook and read to my husband; now I'm trying to dictate into a tiny Sony tape-recorder, state of the art and horribly expensive. The tapes, buttons and push release mechanisms are so small and difficult to work I feel like a surgeon doing open heart surgery on a premature infant, so teensy is the field, so huge and clumsy seem my hands.

Also, now that my husband's law firm is expanding and growing, I have lists of concerns similar to, but more tony and Century City than, PTA meetings and carpools.

Such as: how to say hello, be warm and friendly to all the women lawyers without needing a new pain-killer prescription from my doctor. Besides wearing their power suits, these Century City women attorneys have now developed power grips. I wince when one approaches down the hallway, my hands will soon be crushed in a powerful squeeze—all the little nerves and arthritic joints will be screaming for mercy. We know by now women lawyers have to work harder than men, they have to outdo the old boys' circle after all. The problem is, the cuter and littler they are, the harder they crush. It could be worse; we could have foot squeezing-or-crushing rituals in our society; then would be in deep, deep trouble, for my feet are definitely the most ouchy places of anywhere on my body. Thank God strangers and friends can't press that particular flesh. The youngest and cutest are always the most ferocious hand manglers; I guess they have got the most to prove.

Another problem of hitting the up-market, as my beloved British friends are wont to say, is I can afford to go to school and take subjects that interest me, and have anxiety attacks trying to keep up with the real students. I dabble along trying to juggle too many things.

Yet another problem that comes with a certain degree of affluence is worrying about my car. Now all the years of parking anyplace and throwing everything into my car to run around and do errands with is over. I do not park my Jaguar just anywhere anymore. Certain beaches in Venice are out because of black-leather-motorcycle-hoodlum-types. I used to park my little nondescript former vehicle anywhere and not think twice about it, but I refuse to risk my gleaming gray beauty to tempt iconoclasts. There are many neighborhoods I won't even go into without my husband in his more down-market number. One doesn't want to attract anarchists, of course, so that does restrict me. Yesterday I was scolded by a good friend who looked into my car in which I had been doing errands all day around Beverly Hills—boots to be repaired, sweaters cleaned, books returned—he said, "Elinor, you're treating this elegant car just like it was a Datsun!"

So, I can't do that anymore, although I do think in my own mind of my car like my home or myself, I wasn't expecting company just then! I have to run around in my sweat suit and tennis shoes sometimes 'til I dress up. Sometimes the house is wreck until the cleaning lady comes in. Oh heck, I'm still me; I dislike worrying about appearances all the time. I need time out, I need to trash out, pig out, cool out and slow down it's so relaxing. Ever try it?

NOISE POLLUTION

A whole lot of problems are being spawned by our sybaritic quest of unnatural luxuries like cool food and air-conditioned cars to ensure a cool us. As far as our ancestors were concerned, if you found a berry or a fish, you ate it, licked your lips and considered yourself a lucky guy. It was consumed, no ifs, ands or buts. If you downed something larger, like a moose, you called your family, and friends, often everyone ate till they dropped.

If it was a very large beast, a hairy mastodon mayhap, you got on the jungle drums and tattooed out a message that said "ya'll come, hear?" to the neighbors. After the feast, everyone slept it off till they could regain their mobility. Basically, that about took care of food procurement and dispersal. Skulking hyena and swooping vulture waited in the wings—and that took care of most of cleanup for the bash. Voila, nutrition was accomplished. If there was no berry crop, why, one did not eat berries. One dug for roots, grubbed for tasty insects lodged in holes in trees, which were the pantry, basically, and man was ingenious in harvesting its fruits, by hook, crook or pointed digging stick (see Hannah Daryl in *Clan of the Cave Bear.*)

Cut to a few million years later. Man evolved and just had to have strawberries for Christmas dinner. So he invented the freezer and flash-frozen berries. He got tired of going out to the hunt every single day, so he invented the supermarket. So many people wanted to get to the markets he invented the mall, and then the cars to bring the clan in from far away. He could no longer jump in and out of brooks on his way to forage, so he had to invent a means to cool off in these autos, so he invented air conditioners. Voila, the freon gas used to protect all this sitting meat was unleashed, and in time the ozone layer that protected our planet from too much ultraviolet ray was depleted, and from there came many ills.

Skin cancers increased. The air and water became hotter. Giant hurricanes were spawned in the western hemispheres and cyclones in the eastern ones. Droughts became more common as things heated up, although Bangladesh continued to have its usual killer floods. America became parched, both east and west, north and south. The sun came out in Seattle; the bread basket of the Midwest hardly produced enough loaves for Liechtenstein, let alone the vast United States.

And I, on the eve of my victory in my passionate campaign for peace and quiet in my neighborhood, that is to quiet down or completely eliminate the dreadful racket leaf-blowing gardeners have inflicted on the backyards of the suburbs. If I had wanted to live under the path of the airplanes at LAX or next to a factory, I would have moved there. We wore ourselves to the nib so we could move to this green and peaceful place, only to have this sweet solitude blasted apart every Tuesday and Friday by the infernal machines. Not only is there brain-splitting noise, but the foul fumes actually set off a smoke alarm in my bedroom, and the debris and dried animal feces forced into the air from the blower gave me an asthma attack. Curse these satanic devices! My mission was to have gardeners go back to the rake, the broom and the hose. Then came this drought. Now gardeners feel justified using their blower at blast. What did they do all the years before the blower from hell was invented? They use a rake and their hands. The drought has dried up my hopes of support in the gardening community against these evils…everyone is too worried now that there won't be enough H2O to sustain the plants, let alone to sluice off the driveways.

But I say this is one part of similar rackets in other locales…we are increasingly assaulted at quiet beaches by jet skis roaring through the breakers, how did people get around the shoreline before they were invented? How ever did the kiddies amuse themselves before they souped up their '69 Dodges to cruise Ventura Boulevard?

But, you say, aren't you making an awful big fuss about 20 minutes of blowing twice a week? Aha, I reply, you are forgetting that the neighbors behind, and on two sides of me also have their leaf-blowing banshees, so there is hardly a serene morning or afternoon left in the week.

Walden Pond couldn't have been written, nor would much think-tank quality thoughts be produced in the racket of today's L.A. We have traded our sacred sanctuaries for litter-less lawns, and I say, it's a danged bad trade-off. Let's go back to a little more mulch, ladies and gentlemen, and to not being awakened by a blast from the dad-blamed blowers. It's Tuesday morning, I awake with throbbing temples…dream gone, sinuses on pulse. What a way to start the day.

Maybe we need to pay our gardeners more for the slower methods of old, but restore our neighborhoods to us. Where is the Environmental Protection Agency when you need it most?

NO EXCUSES

You know something? You just can't win. We have more mental health professionals giving us advice individually, on the radio, on T.V, in groups, in offices, in your place or your home. There is almost no place you cannot get some good therapeutic advice by cable satellite, or short wave radio. There are radio headbands for joggers and underwater radios for snorkelers. So you can find out how to improve your personality on land, by sea or in the air.

So how come, then, we are all more insecure about ourselves than ever?

Aha...there's a good answer. As it is, we are bombarded with media attention, mostly negative, about things our grandmother didn't even whisper to their husbands in the dark. We are constantly being urged to sniff, check, worry about, or inspect ourselves for something others might not like or might take some sort of exception to.

In the old days, you were who you were and that was pretty much it. If you were a fat slob, well, what do you expect with a mother like that-just the same. Or an Aunt Edna. Or if your folks were svelte, you must take after your father's side of the family and who knew about them, they fled out of town one step ahead of the sheriff, if your peer at any family long enough, you will come up with a fresser, a horse thief or a genuine fatso somewhere along the way. If all else fails and there are only slim and beautiful ancestors, no problem. Glands. Poor Bubele has overactive glands.

No one could say she didn't, could they? So? Prove me a liar, the defendant could say.

Nowadays, forget it. You are expected to take responsibility for every curve, every ounce and every wrinkle. Fat? How many Jane Fonda workouts have you missed?

Stuck at home with the one month old? Get the tape, that's no excuse. Heredity? So what if you come from a family that toured

Eastern Europe for five generations as *mountain man and kin*, the folks who compete with the Alps for the biggest belt measurements-and win. Doesn't matter. If you had any character at all, you would eat lettuce and prevail over your genes.

There is no excuse for anything any more. Lousy marriage, chuck her out, find a new one. Lousy nose, what are you waiting for? Here are the names of three good plastic surgeons. Too old to change your profession? Nonsense-get a hair implant, lift your eyelids so you look wide awake, check into Georgette Klinger for color added to eyebrows, tresses and lashes. Get a good facial; they'll never know you fought with Teddy at San Juan Hill.

Nothing's a good excuse anymore. You're supposed to write your own script, be your own best friend, and re-parent yourself as well!

MEDITATION ON THE END OF SUMMER

For a month now, my forest of cosmos has been getting shabby. I planted them, half-inches in March, they grew for three months like Topsy, and then flowers broke out in June. The green period was enjoyable, as I speculated on whether each plant would be white, pink or fuchsia colored, and how it would look when mature. Those were quizzical times, each plant mysteriously the same, and inscrutable...only mixed somas come in flats; to know the color, you must wait many months to purchase the mature plant...although I hate surprises in general, (they've never been very good ones) I could take a chance on this low-keyed posy roulette, the stakes were ones I could live with. Three quarter-inch wood from Armstrong's.

In the fullness of time, I had multitudinous reds, pinks, and whites, much fluffy ferny greenery, and a back yard just buzzing with stuff. For, concomitant to the blooming of the cosmos, came a species of bird I saw at no other time of year anywhere, hummingbirds, but had an entirely different M.O. Hummingbirds hovered; these little beasts swooped in, in twos and threes, and settled on the lower twigs of the now bush-like plants, large as hedges some of them were by mid-June.

The cosmos crowded out all the petunias, daisies and roses on the upper deck; no matter, it was really the birds I was after. They zoomed in morning and night, in larger and larger numbers to eat the leaves of the flower like so much radicchio, or endive, if that's too bitter for your taste. Olive, with white or yellow markings shading to puce, these creatures were the height of fashion in the late summer. The problem was, nobody knew what they were. I borrowed a *Fielding's Bird Guide to Southern California*, and scanned the pictures and text. As far as I could ascertain, these guys were either Baltimore warblers, or Robin's warblers. (Usually found in

Nicaragua). I checked and checked again, but yep. The little guys were either way, way off-course, or caught a special out to the coast for the feast. And where in the world were they the rest of the year, I never saw them browse on any other fruit or flower, what was their secret? And did anyone care but me?

I'm sure, reading this, many of you will have had similar experience to bird watching in your own backyard. And maybe just never followed through. Can't reasonable people get together and figure this thing out, I see lots of somas up and down the area, surely others have bird guests, as well?

I've enjoyed the flora and fauna show immensely for three months...however. It's the last day of August, and the plants are getting ratty-looking. I yearn to start some new babies in the garden but there's no room left. And, *quelle douleur*, I'm tired of cosmos. Not of the birds, but of the everlasting cosmos. The damned stuff is as persistent as a weed, and will not quit. I shop in Mordigan's wistfully for blue salvia and marigolds, for...

I cannot touch the plants, for fear of seriously disturbing the beloved little busy, browsing, chirpy occupants. What to do? The cosmos gets heavier, falls over despite all stakes, which have given up the ghost pounds and pounds ago.

One day when my hormones are whippy and I feel testy, I tell the gardeners to take out every other plant!

There it's done. I will prune, pot some, but leave enough of a salad bar to keep the chubby aviarians in their beloved petals, it's done, and the devil take the hindmost. An hour later, sick warblers, I think, congregate and perch together on a branch of an old lemon tree overlooking the most popular of the cosmos graze. They turn their little heads toward each other and chirp away a mile a minute, turning from one to the other, clearly wondering what the hell has happened to their environment.

Clearly a catastrophe. They don't feed on the remaining plants. Now it's six days later, oh, I see one or two lackadaisically smelling a petal or two. But most have gone. Where, I can't imagine.

I truly feel Ludwig of the rain forests. Like the Weyerhaeuser Lumber Company. Like Dow Chemical. In short, folks, I'm on the wrong side of this environmental issue.

Singlehandedly, and selfishly, I have destroyed their world, their pantry, their Eden...oh yes, I know, sooner or later the plants would have to be cut back or removed, but not now. And, no doubt anticipating further atrocities, they have given up on me, and have returned to the Chesapeake area, if not Managua. There to spread the word of this callousness, no doubt.

There was a lot of fog this morning... I have a virus and bronchitis. I always do at the end of summer every year.

YOU'RE ALL WET, ALICE WATERS

Although I'd sworn off nouvelle cuisine (after many a hungry experience) of any and all extractions...French, Texan or Mexican... or any combination of thereof, I had to be in the Bay Area for a conference and was so excited at the prospect of seeing my sons up there, I forgot all hard-won lessons and idiotically made reservations at Chez Panisse in a fit of festivity.

Restaurants throughout the area were packed, tens of other conference-goers enviously offered to take these prized reservations off my hands if I had any second thoughts, and thought of juicy, unthinkably delectable pizzas.

Good old Berkeley! I was so excited when I saw the wooden house on Shattuck, so earthly, so natural. Wooden benches and wildflower bouquets welcomed the weary from L.A. Offspring reminisced about the good old college days, when a pizza here was luxury fit for a pasha.

Did we dine...did we ever! But not how I had remembered from my previous experience upstairs, without reservations.

First in the prix fixe offering there was a radicchio platelet with (naturally) raspberry vinaigrette and (obviously) walnut oil dressing. Then there was another plate of greens with some bloody squab nestled within, plucked from the rooftops, no doubt and stuffed, I suspect, with their own droppings. Wrapped in their own nests? What a delicacy.

The main course was raw pork, basted with gefilte fish lacking only an oink and an *oy vey* from a rabbi to qualify as a genuine sacrilege. In my youthful enthusiasm, I had completely repressed the most vile of nouvelle's many detestations...and that being even decent food was transmogrified into garbage by dint of being under...if you were lucky.. And *un-done* if you weren't. Every fish is sushied, and all beef tartared.

San Francisco eateries are famous for peculiarity and panache; but there is a limit to *avant garde* past which I do not care to *avanti*. This meal was so stylish it was positively unwholesome; right down to and including our waiter the very arch Bernard, so pale of face and lethargic we feared for his immune system.

It happened to be an unseasonably hot night, and between the snail-slow services of a terminally effete Bernard and our over-vinegared insides, "flag down that waiter" was the byword of the evening, as he kept the pitcher of water tantalizingly far from our reach.

The *denoument* of the dinner was a chocolate cookie and pureed raspberries for dessert, which defied ruination.

We staggered out, sickened and starved, too demoralized by disappointment to stop in for a big Mac. The ride home was quiet, each of us wondering whether it would be pitticoris, AIDS or trichinosis that would polish us off.

I bet Alice Waters never ate any of this garbage; she is probably laughing herself sick over gullible "foodies" who pay to get starved and grossed out, while she enjoys a repast of well-roasted leg of lamb and well-baked potatoes.

Copies of this restaurant review to the Board of Health, if you please.

SHAMPOOARAMA

Recent ads have stated that hair gets the blahs, gets bored and limp with the sameness, the ineffable tiresomeness of a one-shampoo diet. Now, how would you like to eat only one food, say, corn on the cob or hot pastrami for the rest of your life—relentlessly for ever and ever? Well, evidently that's the way hair feels—it gets bored stiff or bored limp or bored straggly, according to your type.

So I stopped into my local drug and health food store and came home with a feast—a feast for the old hair follicles. What did I buy? Well, the standard balsam shampoo and conditioner, some far away Aussie Moist (love the little kangaroos running around the plastic bottle), and for the practical generic brand, Russell Travis Shampoo. That's so you can just be plebian—one of the folks.

Then there's Elemental Sea Green (seaweed and vitamin E.) And there are shampoos for screwballs, Queen Bee Shampoo, to keep you young forever and to make your hair extremely fertile; olive oil and honey shampoo with a vitamin E base for you believers in vitamins, and there's Camomile Shampoo for those of you who are believers in herbs (there's also peppermint.) Seriously, sometimes my hair turned out fat and sassy, sometimes conditioned to a state of well, if it had been muscle instead of hair, it would be Bruce Jenner or John McEnroe.

Sometimes it was Jennifer O'Neil on a good day or Tina Turner on a bad one. Sometimes I looked like Grace Jones and one day last week it was Miami Vice!

Well, sometimes (if my hair were a new computer), I'd be a Leading Edge and sometimes I'd be a little dumb and klutzy Macintosh mouse. Oh yes, the true screwball brand of them all was Ogilvie Shampoo with hot oil pearls. This was the weirdest one of all. I used it back east last week where the water is much softer than our L.A water. I thought the hot oil treatment would really help my hair out as I was in the sea swimming for hours everyday. So I've learned that hair gets sunburned and needs help, revitalization and moisturizing.

I used the shampoo as directed; that is, I lathered and rinsed, rinsed, rinsed, lathered some more and rinsed, rinsed, rinsed, got out of the shower and felt my hair; it was still soapy. I get back in, more rinsing and serious fluffing up under the water, parting it, turning my head this way and back, getting particularly the back of my hair and my ears well rinsed, was positive there would not be a scintilla more of soap. *Wrong*! I dried myself all over; got a towel around me and sat in the sun on the balcony to dry my hair—*egads*—more suds appeared. Got a glass, rinsed my hair in the sink, no soap or rather—still soap! Sudsing and sudsing, this shampoo had a hex on it. I gave up. Later that evening, I picked little dried gelatin capsules off my cheeks and off my hairline. The little capsules never dissolved—this was weird in Miami Beach!—and there it dried and stayed high, wide and handsome. It was as if I had cleaned and moussed it all in one step—a really new first for me to this style. My gosh, I felt sticky as heck but I sure looked like a current Elizabeth Taylor going out on the town in Miami Beach last week. All I needed was Don Johnson in his glad rags. I was so intrigued by this turn of events, I tried it again the next night thinking surely the water hadn't been hot enough to get the hot oil and gelatin capsule pearls out. Same non-stop, non-rinse sudsing story, same dry gelatin pearls afterward. They had surely goofed at Ogilvie. I was going to send the bottle back with the rest of the shampoo and explain my story, but I knew they would never believe it so I left the bottle of shampoo in Key Largo when I left, and instead decided to write it up in this believe-it-or-not fashion. I just hope some innocent bunny rabbit didn't give up its life for this ding-dong product. You know how they're always testing cosmetics on poor imprisoned rabbits—this dreadful thing. My hair and I are back to Neutrogena Shampoo plus Wella Conditioner.

We've decided to go mainstream again—both of us are well enough nourished by now to survive and I am staying away from weird shampoos for awhile. I may not have found the fountain of youth, but I certainly found the fountain of suds in Miami last week.

SNORKELING ADVENTURES

While snorkeling in from some deep reefs to the shallows, where I can maneuver into the boat again, I glide over what must be the world's master hatchery peeking through their rind of sand. I see two sea slugs—one an infant —the other a Grandpa Albino.

There are also rare white dolphins off this island.

Suli points out a big ray—I miss it. Hub points out some flying fish—I miss them looking for ray.

Hub has gone off to Douglas Island to chat and to be taken on an epic hunt for the giant Triton's Trumpet, which is the Holy Grail—his Excalibur and his folly.

Our bure comes supplied with everything —or almost everything one could wish for.

Hub has none of his recurrent mysterious tingling symptoms on this trip—but my anxieties persist even in this idyllic spot.

Really—suggests something biological—for sure, doesn't it?

Before this MS gets washed away, too blurred by salt water for anyone, even me to read— I'll ask Noel to Xerox and send a copy home. In case we—or it—do not make it.

FISH STORIES

My first swim to the gazebo reef. It's been a fairly long swim—you have to cover a wide stretch of barren bottom—a beige world: sand, bleached animal and vegetable matter—even the fish are beige here. Then a long stretch of tundra—grasslands, dappled and quivering in the pale green eddies of warm water. Sun and tundra-dazzled fish dart around here almost perfectly camouflaged from predators. Which so far, I notice, is only me.

I glide above my favorite fish that's lit from inside—reminds me of nothing so much as the Alka-Seltzer ad where the guy has a three-alarm fire burning in his tum after too much Mexican food. I follow this fellow as far as I can to see his incredible make-up trick. But he darts under a ledge of coral. I can imagine the menacing sight I make, eagle-spread above him like a killer whale. This same defense is taken by a herd of small royal-blue/purple/cobalt ones.

My only problem in this sweet, sweet place is deciding which fish are my favorites. Right now, although it's a tough choice—past of waving sea grass out among the coral are various–sized reef fish, darting about showing off zigs and zags of blue, violet, and peacock. They are, I think, best. Because unique to this time and place, where everything is just a little different from their cousins from other islands.

Reminds me of Ray Bradbury's story of a traveler back in time who accidentally steps off the requisite path for the time travelers and crushes a plant or two while regaining his footing. When he returns to his present—the spelling is slightly different—also the current politics and government are different. Just like these fish. Yes, your same basic fish shape, but with many subtle differences here in Fiji.

My designated favorites swim around with little dazzles of color, until I get directly overhead—a great big unknown and possibly dangerous new fish of some kind?

Then they settle deep to the branches of some stag coral—quivering and pulsing.

Sad to be throwing these beloved jewels of the reef into such a fearful state—I swim on, considerably slowed down by H's big blue shirt which I am swimming in to ward off sun poisoning—cuffs dangling floppily around my hands.

Oh, what about sea-grapes? Snorkeling with Suli yesterday, I saw green grape-like clusters on the floor of the sea; I told him they looked just like green grapes we eat at home. He said yes, they are good to eat—I ate some. The salt water flavored and obscured whatever they would have tasted like dry—but I liked harvesting fresh produce off the ocean floor.

I write: to avoid Freud.

I write: to avoid life.

I write: to enhance life.

I write: to circumvent death. I don't mind dying—I just don't want to be annihilated.

Of course, dying is easy; getting published is hard!

What's become of me? Anything?

Questionnaire to follow.

I'm going to read Freud now—I have to make this notebook last till I'm out of Micronesia. Out of Micronesia—I think Isak Dinesen's already done that.

Africa is easy; Micronesia is hard.

Saturday, December 21. I spend my time on Forbes Fabled Fiji Island:

A. Reading back copies of *Forbes Magazine*—never have I considered the option one has so open. Actually, the thing of interest in them is that so many people want to spend their lives optioning out, counseling numbers, amortizing and planning their next takeover. I really like the quotes on the back page; little gems of financial wisdom.

B. Reading Sigmund Freud.

C. Applying either suntan lotion, or bug spray, or both. Then, washing it off.

D. Swimming off the reef.

Lunch turns out to be mostly frozen! With our front yard a-wiggle with Pesca, we eat mushy lobster tail from Australia and frozen veggies—what happened to the fabled vegetable garden?

I'm sorry to say the chef also has a heavy hand with the pastry. My husband's blow fish *en croute* resembled nothing so much as a sardine encased in a tank, so impervious to knife and fork was that crust. Oh well—Onissimo has lots of time to get it right. It's close to Christmas: I think he's homesick for his home on a neighboring island—all of which have—trust me—unpronounceable names. They look difficult in English, but this is not the half of it—since many letters are pronounced differently in Fiji.

The people seem happy, each family in its new little building. Forbes is running this island rather like an ideal society. The place is an old-fashioned copra plantation, where the coconut is still chopped and processed for its oil, used in making soaps, cosmetics and cooking oil. This operation no longer pays for itself—but Forbes apparently hopes it may come back—and wishes to retain employment for the natives and to preserve the old ways. He supplies everything to the island people—homes, fuel, doctors, nurses and schooling.

In return, they keep the place spruced up—they work at gardening, plumbing, building, housekeeping and boat-tending.

There are herds of cows rambling aimlessly around the island. This morning, the boat took Hubby shelling—and me fish-watching around the far aside on the island, where I saw about two dozen cows resting on a beach, under some trees. That was a new one on me, beach-going cows.

The days are flying fast—soon we'll have to pack it in and move on, and we know how I love that!

Hub has had his second-finest shelling day ever. He has caught—live, I fear—cowries, cones, top shells, spider, conch, giant clams, olives and frog shells. His finest shelling, he tells me, was in Captive, Florida, kidnapping unwary giant conch from the tepid seas. (Then to Key West; that's where we should have invested in Mel Fischer's treasure hunt. He was pitching for funds—shortly afterward he hit it big. Oh well.)

One nice thing around here—one tends to go native quite fast. No shoes, no bathing suit and no tight bras.

Living here would be nice. No one diets, works out or worries about looks. No lipstick. Dress-up is flowers in the hair, and a clean *shmata* tied at the front—known as *pareau* in Tahiti.

That's what these idylls are intended to give to us—the very temporary experience of what it's like to live like a *raj*.

A few weeks—then back to the working classes for us.

We wing out of here tomorrow on the plane *Capitalist Tool* to Suva, there to catch Qantas to Heron Island on the Great Barrier Reef—H's dream island (he fervently hopes).

9:30—my eyes are closing—I guess from all the sun and swimming. That's all for now.

NEIL DOUGLAS TO PLANTATION MANAGER?

These Douglass's once owned everything around here. Their Scottish ancestors settled in these islands in the 1850's and have been here ever since. They look and sound very British—the children, however, sound like the locals speaking Pidgin English—since they've grown up with the local children.

Flora, the wife of Noel Douglass, who is very Scottish even after many generations in these equatorial parts, is an interesting mix. She, too, has British ancestors from Edinborough and is prototypically English: small porcelain figures all over her house—plus a little Pekinese dog which she carries around and kisses on the mouth. She would be a perfect Brighton Beach hotel owner—eccentric and traditional. Except for one thing: her eyes are anything but English—they are almost totally brown—only an almost imperceptible white bit outlines the brown iris. You see—her grandmother is pure Polynesian.

She also has a very un-English gift for seeing the future in visions. She's matter-of-fact about it, although the scary visions disturb her dreadfully—and she hates being laughed at for her precognition.

It certainly makes sense to me that the brain, which we know can emit alpha, beta, gamma and many other waves—has energy patterns and capabilities—more or less pronounced that we have not yet named and quantified.

Common dogs and cats can pick up more kinds of smells, sounds, and emotional vibes than most of us more advanced types.

There are certain groups of people that seem specifically gifted: whole populations of them. I'm not sure this is a gift—or a punishment, really.

The news bringer of death and of disaster is not loved.

More uncommon animals, like sharks, whales, and porpoises have detection systems we are just starting to fully investigate.

Horses, grizzly bears and large cats can pick up when we fear them; from, I imagine, a combination of scent changes (or possibly the amount of sweat) and postural changes.

NAMING

My older son has adopted two street puppies which we went to see last weekend, when they were eight weeks old. One looked vaguely beagle-ish, the other a perfect "Our Gang" kind of character, roguish and ready to join in every and any activity. Brave and intelligent, the animals stole my heart by the end of the weekend.

Their given names, Jake and Alice, soon became too tame for their antics, and so I devised other more appropriate designations. Josh's girlfriend was telling us about hearing from an old college friend, a Polish lad by the name of Anton Dryzwycky, pronounced Drizzwicky. I looked at Jake prancing in dizzying circles around the sofa after little Allie and her nyla-chew, his one black eye and general mutt-in-the-manger appearance and decided he looked exactly like a Dryzwycky, whatever that was. The natural companion for such a one was, naturally enough, another *mittel*-European designation. She became Hasenpfeffer, a German endearment and Hasenpfeffer it was then, till the nipping began. I was a little afraid of these characters, babies though they are, because of their obvious lineage which is supposed to be largely boxer. She does have a little square face, but he looks like a baby pit bull, only prettier. My son admitted the folks said his dad was a pit bull. Jake likes to nip my cheek, and I am not used to little needle teeth taking the Lancôme blusher off my face, particularly since I do not have any references in his portfolio, nor the relative facts on his resume and do not know his make at the local police station. Could be he comes from a criminal background.

He was one of ten pups in the litter, and my son picked him out of a shopping car outside a market in San Francisco's tenderloin district...without a pedigree, one didn't know the legal status of his forebears (maybe a con artist or two)?

He is an engaging little fellow, with his one dark eye. She is more quiet, but likes to bite on hands. Sharkey, Snarkey and Barkey come rapidly to mind when I gaze into her eyes. She was the first to learn to bark, and she has a disconcerting habit of not looking me in the eye when I hold her up. I suspect abuse of some sort, she should be more trusting. Of course, she was the runt of the litter, so maybe life taught her some bitter lessons about supply and demand. Nevertheless, she conducted herself reasonably well when dealing with new people (who may or may not covet her share of the family nutritional supplies). She has two black eyes and better balanced coloring, she looks a lot classier than her litter-mate, i.e. she has more boxer in her—more your standard household pooch than the terror of the neighborhood.

Jake is the quintessential mutt, a true Heinz 57 chap from the streets, with the many sterling qualities this lineage allows. They are not overbred…nervous and jumpy. Instead they are intelligent, lively and very independent, since both my son and his girlfriend (and future wife) work all day, the dogs are left mostly on their own and have really been splendid about trying to do the right thing, carpet and upholstery-wise. They are reported to be very brave when getting their puppy shots, and extremely loyal in relationship to sharing toys and chews with each other, although they do tend to get carried away at the beach and want to follow and go home with everyone who exclaims over them, "aren't they adorable little pit bulls?"

I got very worried about their ancestry showing up later and purchased a small book detailing pit bull characteristics and I am vastly reassured that they are a much maligned breed, abused by certain misguided elements in the name of sport or security.

They are widely famed as patient with children, and never ever turning on their own master, large or small. I've grown to love little drizzle puss and puppy wampums. My affection is mostly expressed in the ever-changing nicknames I devise for them. I've not spent time around very young animals, and I find this silly baby phase to be enchanting. Of course, I am a guest in their home, and do not clean up after them. But I have bought puppy training books in case they are left with us when the kids go off on vacation. They all live in San Francisco; what a rehearsal for the real thing, grandchildren, I mean. Of course, if that doesn't happen, I may have to read more about boxer, beagle and other breeds, and make do with the furry family members I have.

It wouldn't hurt to buy some stock in U.S. Air, either.

NAME CALLING

About affectionate appellation in the U.K.; it really is true that people in the same family, at any rate, do call their spouses darling. Also their grown sons, the cat, and the girl who brings tea. I'll be darned if I didn't think it was only in Los Angeles environs that the British such as Tallulah Bankhead (and an occasional other such as Zsa Zsa) who customarily did this—but evidently no. It is widespread and upper class. The lower ones of course call each other ducks, luv (pronounced loov) and dearie. Did you know it was authentic?

Just as they really say ta for thanks; ciao in Rome.

They are rightfully aware and receptive to this nuance in the famous *Cats* score.

Other lovely appellations: Madam. At home, it is so phony, so obviously cadged from the continent. Here in London it's just lovely. I feel so respected and upper class at the Goring—a lovely hotel where service is scintillating!

MAINTENANCE

I looked forward to a driving trip, where I would have an easy time packing, since I could just throw the bags in the back of the car, and not have to plan so carefully, *and* have everything I could want or need with me.

When I prepare to travel either for long or short trips, I am confronted by the fact that, on this my fifth decade on earth, there is precious little of me that doesn't need what, if I were a '68 Pontiac, would amount to a total detailing, *every* day. Hardly any of me is just right--neither too moist nor too dry.

There are a number of appliances that have been miniaturized for the sake of convenience, and without which one is exhorted never to leave home. I have unwisely fallen into some of these capitalistic traps and have made purchases that I thought would enhance me when I sallied forth to meet the world and its inhabitants, face to face. I hoped not to meet it wrinkle to wrinkle, hence the many little machines to smooth and freshen, to shine and sharpen brain, mind and teeth. My God, the anxieties travelers used to have are as nothing compared with modern cares. In times gone by, you wondered a bit if you would be felled by a cannibal, shark or mountain grizzly when you set out from the safety of your own igloo, teepee or log cabin to tread the fearsome wastelands of western America. At least then, whatever was going to assault you generally made quick work of it, so it was a much more anxious dread, not a psychological cold war that gave you palpitations of fear when there was no direct predator bearing (or baring) down. I tell you, progress has advanced the arts of dread, paranoia and hypochondria to such a state that no one dares to stir abroad without a vial of breath spray or crotch deodorant, lest he should meet his own coach-class Madonna. In Grandma's Day, if you lived through the blizzards and the grizzly bear was on a diet that day, why, you were right as rain. Now, *The New York Times* has come to L.A., and on every science day, we read of the hazards of too much indulgence in sun, sea and feasting, things which were considered unalloyed blessings in Granny's times. Death lurks everywhere, according to modern scientists. Weren't we better off without microscopes? Fresh water looked good and tasted good, so it was good. No one wondered if dreaded staph or fatal amoebic dysentery swam in every sip. If you croaked afterwards, you never connected it with the fatal beverage.

Oh, the scrubbing, boiling, defoliating, the waxing, painting and pore vacuuming. The rinsing, flossing, brushing, dredging. The label reading, calorie counting, nutritionist consulting. Oh my God, can cholesterol be much worse than this ordeal? Everything has its own sponsor and spokesman; attention is paid not only to body parts, but to areas *between* body parts. Space between toes and teeth serviced by Tinactin and waxed dental floss...can you imagine areas between areas having their very own products and pharmacopeias? Tinactin and dental floss would have made Grandma, not to mention the grizzly bear, laugh themselves silly. Well, I am not going anywhere unless all this stuff comes too. Fungal spores must be subdued. Plaque scraped off the sides of teeth. Bottom teeth must be retained at night, TMJ warded off with one's Lucite prosthetic retainer, custom-made, natch. A bit of spontaneity certainly has disappeared, but I refuse to lollygag around the world without my pill box, after all, estrogen levels must be kept up and osteoporosis kept at bay. *N'est ce pas?*

Innards have their own granules providing moisture and bulk, God forbid we forget the Metamucil, and naturally, oat bran is hauled along everywhere, you want I should develop dangerous arterial buildup? God, the crisps, fibers, and veggies that are bundles up in baggies for the road. Now we provide preparations and nostrums for almost any unmentionable anywhere on the chassis, fore or aft, inside or out, public or private.

One can take along gimmicks, devices and even one's laptop to record vital statistics and log of critical functions. Why, a friend of mine goes nowhere without her motivational weight loss tapes, a set of 16 in a plastic carrying case, plus all the freeze-dried, low-salt, low-calorie items she will need to eat for the days of her trip. I don't really believe she gets to see or do much besides her program on these trips. She likes to hear the hypnotic music, research data, exhortations, chanting that is supposed to soothe and regulate her subconscious productions. Highway One was getting pretty scary and phobia-producing; he let me listen to them as we skidded around hairpin curves like Mario Andretti meets the Fonz.

Fortunately, the road was so scary—California Highway One—that it scared all the plaque off my teeth and all the cholesterol out of my arteries. So there. You can take me anywhere.

REMODEL

Great day in the morning! What morning? Well, July 29—a humdrum date, you say. Not at all, it feels like my birthday to me.

Anyone know why might that be? Today, I'll have you know, I learned I can communicate in another language. Yes, honestly, the recipient of a heretofore indecipherable set of grunts and muffled harrumphing's now understands every syllable of my strangled message.

Who was this, and why was I expounding in Strangelese? Of course, it was my dentist, and I was attempting to communicate through the drain...that is, four large rolls of cotton wadding to dry up my saliva. And, I was still able to have all my questions answered by my (possibly telepathic) oral healer.

Wow, is he ever a whiz. I tell you my statement was more akin to Raquel Welch in *One Million B.C.*, more Paleolithic than any modern tongue, I did not expect to be understood, so was I astonished when he grokked.

I was having my toofers resurfaced this hot summer morning and feeling more like an urban renewal project that not, while patiently submitting to two hours of scraping and refilling the potholes in my bonded front toofers.

So I didn't really expect him to answer the query, "How is your boy enjoying summer camp this year?"

"How come you don't have screens yet? The bugs stay out of your office even with open windows?" and, "Why are there yellow spots on some of my teeth?"

All my cottony, desiccated queries were answered calmly and rapidly. I thought I sounded like Flipper, babbling away in strange, cetacean tones, but evidently, he understands Dolphin.

Emerged from this primitive exchange with twinkling choppers. They were to the old bonded resigned one what the iron-coated

Merrimack would be to new fiberglass Hovercrafts; I surveyed my porcelain front six teeth.

Eureka...just like being dipped into the fountain of youth, snout first! Lost a good 30 years from the front of my mouth. Could be the gnawing edge of a Dewey 16 year old, I exulted. A wish, a plea rose from the depths—-by God, if they can restore the pearly whiteness of the old canines, why the heck can't they work on the rest of me?! If they could only smooth, re-plane, and re-contour lots more of me...would that be great or what?

I want to straighten out everything from chin to metatarsals. From dorsal plane to lateral. From stem to stern (and back again). From beam to bridge. From starboard to port, mainsail to topsail. You get the picture.

Who knows maybe science will come up with an analogue to porcelain for the flesh, why not? They have artificial blood, hearts, kidneys, are artificial skin and flesh far behind?

If it won't hurt any more than this procedure, and in turn are selling, remembering my one shot rule, of course. If it takes more than one injection of anything, no deal. I'll wait longer for the laser, or other space age stuff.

In other words, you can zap, light, or blip me. But don't make a mark on my skin! No hospital check-ins. I want to see curtains blowing in an open window, I want to be awake, and I want to be out in time for lunch.

I am an old Star Trekkie and we know miracles are right around the corner. My proof ? Have you seen any klingons bothering you lately? I thought not.

LO-TECH-LADY IN A (EARLY 80`S) LOW-TECH WORLD

Myself, I don't truly believe man was meant to cook with high frequency radio waves that get beamed out of an oven, thereby generating the heat that cooks my sliced carrots. Yes, I've had quite a lot of success with carrots and some green beans. True. The rest of my microwave cooking has been at a humble level that would cause Julia Child to scoff. Yes, scoff. Mainly I've heated up yesterday's oatmeal and spaghetti, turned out pretty well.

Everything else has been a disaster. Tried some chicken...it came out looking even deader than when it went in. One of my guests threw up, the other one turned instant vegetarian, and the rest went on strict diets. Every course came out tough, white, stringy and probably carcinogenic, whether it's supposed to be cheese, fowl, fish or cauliflower. One friend swears you have to leave the food untouched for seven minutes until the molecules quit jumping around or you get really messed up. The kids think anything that emerges from the oven will give you cancer and would rather take a swim in the Love Canal than eat my broccoli.

The machine is unreliable...even frozen stuff comes out still icy in places and hot in others, if you don't remember to turn it. Weird.

The one thing it's great for is cooking to lose a lot of weight. There is only so much crunching my elderly jaws and teeth can manage in one day. As it is, it takes me an hour and a half to much up my noontime meal—by dinner I'm exhausted and need lots of veggies to fill up but not out. Hence: the microwave.

My nutritionist actually talked me into it...after being totally opposed to one for at least ten years. Because I don't like machines, and more important, machines don't like me. I'm real happy I can drive and type up my own stuff.

Some things I can do but not reliably are: work the video, the sun-powered calculator or our new stereo. Usually there's one little part of it I can't quite remember, so the show we want to watch later may or may not be saved. It's always a crap shoot with me.

So, when one has been enjoined from the local Häagen-Dazs and pizza parlor, when Chin-Chin's dumplings are taboo, when one is no longer a see-er at See's, draconian measures must certainly be taken. My gourmet license has expired, and my taste buds impounded. No goulash, no mu shu pork, no spring roll for me. Internationally, I've been neutralized.

Pushed to my breaking point, I went out and purchased the microwave and a computer. (Even though I just hate it when my machines are smarter than I am.)

I'm up to "rutabagas" in my microwave skills, and up to "centering" on my computer. If I stick around long enough, they'll have perfected the speak-to model instead of the type-in one, and at last, I'll take up literature other than "You and Your Professional Word Writer." *That* will be good.

My finest comment as a microwave cook comes from a five-month old whose mother asked me to please give her bottle of soy milk, "40 seconds in the microwave." Baby Anne drank every drop of her perfectly warmed milk contentedly and dropped off to sleep soon afterwards, leaving her mother and me to chat in peace. My best critique by far. I'm happy with small triumphs, it would seem. Too out of it to be able to learn.

But I was told sit down, turn on machine, punch in one and start. So I typed for an hour, making many, many mistakes; but thrilled at no return, no page endings. I was thrilled. I was creative. I got tired.

Unsure of what to do next, I figured well, can't figure it out so I'll turn it off and get instructions later. Hah. Little did I know the stupid machine needed to be explicitly told to "save it". Why in the universe would I spend an hour writing if I didn't want to keep it?

I think the machines hate me. Or at least my writing style. Not an auspicious beginning. Was telling the infernal machine—which I hope to learn to love—I am writing not for myself only. Not to fit into the little categories the computer program now wants me to.

Boy have I been down—I've gone seven rounds with my current virus. So far: It's been a sweeping K.O. Virus, 7; *me,* 0. Zip. I can't shake the wheezing, the weakness, the insomnia, the coughing, the shallow pained breath—and the fear of having permanent asthma.

The world looks black at the moment. And the newspaper and TV sure as hell don't help; in fact, for a few days I was too sick to stand hearing about earthquakes, melting polar caps that will eventually flood out my new carpets, revolution creeping up to our door as the Russians start out P.R.'ing and out-cute-ing R.R. himself. That's the King of Personality, Ronnie himself.

And even Channel 6 saw a wonderful *Discovery* that showed huge green sea turtles body-surfing in at high tide, laboriously laying eggs which are mostly eaten as they are laid. The babies hatch out, have to scramble up through perhaps a foot of sand to get to the air; figure out which way the sea lies—and *then* get picked off one by one by a vast army of birds, lizards, crabs—and at water's edge—more turtles surfing in to lay eggs. Many die of heat and dehydration at the very edge of the blessed water itself. Once in their proper element, the sea, many cruel cruising fins announce the sea predators are ready to take their turn. Poor little valiant hatchlings—what a murderous welcome into this world. As soon as they are hatched, they're considered mere prey! How they live, what they eat is totally unknown. Maybe just as well, maybe they *feel* very little and are not very conscious and aware. Let's hope with those mothers who lumber right over them as the babies make their desperate scramble to the sea; as we're holding our breath. Not even as food for another species. There must be a point for everyone when they say, "oh, what's the use, anyway?" I'm struggling to follow doctor's instructions, watch my weight and cholesterol.

OVER 60, OVERWORKED, OVER THE HILL

Got a diagnosis? I get zapped out of my mind about every other week, have for a year now. Blown sky-high, hit the wall, new time zone, flying high and wide. Bombed, stoned, zonked, and blown away. Heart in my throat, all pulses pounding, I lay wide awake, eyes can't even close, till 3, 4, in the a.m. This is not insomnia, this is mania.

What is my problem, drug addiction, psychosis?

None of the above. My idiosyncratic response to the cortisone: I have to take to control my sinuses and asthma.

Do I enjoy these wild altered-state experiences? No way. How people stand having all their faculties letting them down and feeling and doing weird things…is beyond me. I'll take my moods and states *au naturel*, whatever they are, at least they're my own, and not chemically induced.

Love wine and liquor, but not the effects. As Sinatra said, hate California, it's cold and it's damp. When we moved here 30 years ago we thought it was like Hawaii, now we have to go there in the winter to avoid the freezing cold weather here.

With the advance of the years, it's getting harder and harder to fit a life and career around doctors' visits and doctors' homework. It used to be, in the old days (we walk on water and heal you), doctors asked you to comply with their orders, basically, and they did the rest to you. Treatments were carried out in the sanatorium if normal home care didn't do it, they supplied the pills you swallowed, or in the rare case when leeches or machinery was necessary, *it was basically done unto you*. You got to suffer, they got to be omniscient.

The contract stood: you did what you were told; they took the responsibility for it all. If the case turned out badly, your time was up. They assisted at the terminal stages, or handed you over to a white-garbed nurse for sympathy and clean sheets. The nurse was admired insofar as her patient was neat, clean, well-watered and souped, and decent. That was it. The doc was God's assistant, but it was all ultimately up to the big boss.

No more. Now docs are fairly diffident with their advice, tentative, vague. Disease may or may not progress; limbs may or may not heal well, *depending on how you, the patient, conduct yourself.*

It is the age of mammoth lawsuits, thus the age of patient, you brought it all on yourself by your lousy lifestyle and/or non-compliance with "suggestions" It's the age of "listen to your body" instead of do this, do that.

Homework is about all the medical profession promises you.

In other words, a redo of the age-old wisdom of God, the doc helps those who help themselves. (And if you don't, let it be on your head.) We are expert witnesses, not gurus. Advice and consent is about it. No guarantees, don't call us, we'll call you. No longer a hands on affair, it's now laissez-faire between doctor and patient; if he smokes, we may well fire him. Icons are crashing from pedestals all over the land.

I am hard pressed to do anything but be cooperative with the following instructions which leave me about 14 minutes to myself in any given day…

1. ENT man wants me to take lots of long hot showers to clear out sinuses and moisturize lungs so I don't dry up and develop pneumonia which I have been coming down with recently. Compliance with this one directly countermands orders from the DWP to drastically knock down the water consumption. Also causes me guilt feelings about hogging water during the drought. Stress at being a good patient at the cost of being a bad citizen.

2. Restoration dentist wants me to work on my jaw muscles, to realign and strengthen fit of new bridge. With caps on molars, the musculature of the jaw has to be adjusted. 25 minutes a day.

3. Gynecologist *strongly* advises muscle work for the p.g. muscles that hold certain vital organs in place and prevent untoward happenings of the damp variety. 25 minutes a day. Electrical apparatus available and purchased for a small fortune. (It does the contracting and squeezing of that aforementioned muscle for you… worth every cent. Named Miccogyn.)

4. Physical therapist recommends pressing against leather, best around ankles to correct back weakness and pain. 15 minutes, five sets, five reps of each.

5. Same physical therapist insists on weight and pulley contraption to build up shoulder muscles to prevent pinched nerves, sprains and strains there; this was the presenting symptom with him.

6. Periodontist threatens dire degrees of gingivitis and tooth loss if routine from hell not complied with. Patient and not-so-patient oral hygenicists have taught, or tried to teach me, the finer points of wielding the gum stimulator, the dental floss both plain and minted, the proxy-mini, end, soft and regular brushes. The KamGel and the Perodex. When I travel, I need an entourage to carry my equipment. Rembrandt paste and whitener liquids, solids and their dispensers are optional, but recommended.

7. Internist/Cardiologist advises 30 to 45 minute walk a day for health of arteries and such.

8. Nutritionist intones against processed anything and not eating at normal mealtimes *if you are not hungry.* That means often one is not eating when others are, and forced to scrounge up fuel for oneself when everyone else is kayaking or lugeing…

This concludes my treatise. I ask you, is there life after health?

Who has time?

WHAT'S NOW ANYWAY

To the question "What's now?", "What's hot?" or "What's happening?" the answer, I've discovered, definitely depends on your age group/energy level and/or marital status. If you are young and amorous, you probably want to know about your "fave" heartthrobs, if older like me, you may just want to know why your gums throb. *People Magazine* and *Entertainment Tonight* will keep you up to date on the doings of that hunk, or hunkess, with the gorgeous curves and flashing smile. (Sure, *their* teeth are very firmly implanted in their rock-solid gums and jawbones.) I, on the other hand, am going to teach you what's very important for the practical, little bitty nitty gritties of life, namely: mastication.

To the forties-something crowd, what's now may mean what's cooking with Tom Selleck…how's he looking, what is his new baby like, what movie will he do next…(When's he breaking up with his wife?) Peter Horton may be the heartthrob of the thirties-something women: Rob Lowe to the twenties-something ones. Jason Bateman to the teens, and Brian Bonsall to the single digit fans. (They are starting to glamorize movie and television stars in their *months…* like the tiny toddlers, Mary Beth/Kate Olsen, the stars of *Full House*, channel seven Friday nights at 8:30, has been since before they could talk! Now babies will be able to have their role model, glamour girl- or- boy too).

Those of us in our fifty-somethings, whose teeth are getting a little wobbly and besides flabby hips are developing flabby gums pockets measuring more than a four (the periodontal equivalent catastrophe to an eight-point rating on the Richter earthquake scale) are having intense relationships with our periodontists. Yep, I'm learning more than I ever wanted to know about the wide, wide world of gum tissue, its problems, assets and maintenance. Naturally I'm into it because in a sneaky, totally silent way, mine have been letting me down little by little, without so much as a hint, until I found myself with a raging gum infection, on vacation. Fortunately, an excellent dentist was on hand (love Hawaii for that reason), and he promptly declared my gum line a worse ecological disaster than Prince William's Sound! How could this be? I had been a dedicated visitor to dentists, brusher, flosser, even a sheller out of shekels for such fripperies as Water Piks, Interplax toothbrushes and many liters of mouthwash to ensure gingival magnificence. It didn't compute.

Oh but it did, says my gum line guru as he and a veritable squadron of technicians in his Bedford Drive office set about, in a flurry of serried appointments, to acquaint me with the topography of my mouth. We did a whole lot of jawing, with the result that I now have a regime that would put an Olympic athlete to shame. I have to do obeisance to my dental cult a lot more than that: ten minutes at the bathroom sink, forty more on land, sea and air... while watching TV, in my car, talking on the phone and God knows where else to keep my sparkling choppers safely embedded within my very own skull. The way I understand it, it's pretty much do this drill or end up on line behind Martha Raye buying new peppermint Poli-grip.

To help me avoid this outcome, I am educated and sent on my way with a bagful of little instruments from hell. Included are items I never imagined in my worst nightmares. See, the whole idea is that you must disrupt, *break up* the action of the dreaded plaque bacteria before it can mesh together, in precisely twelve hours, to weave a lethal tapestry that emits more toxins from its bacteria than the Love Canal on its worst day. Once it releases that old woofing and warping *stuff* in your mouth that gets together on your unfortunate molars, well, you may as well kiss your toothies bye-bye...your mouth becomes filled with a concrete substance they have to jackhammer loose, and then shovel out by the truckload.

I looked at my new armamentarium: tiny mirror, rubber ice-picks, green floss holder, gels, rinses, swabs, little bottle brushes called proxibrushes you are supposed to scrub between your teeth with. *Sure* I am. That's like telling me to gently insert a sword in one ear, out the other, to clear my mind-without damaging anything! Right. *It won't fit, I tell you.*

There are fresh toothbrushes with which I am supposed to perform fancy stunts, at a 45 degree angle, near my gum line; if I had that much hand-eye coordination, I'd be playing for the Harlem

Globetrotters and making millions. Oh, and don't forget to brush the inside of the cheek and the tongue? The tongue?

Then after all this, you press with the rubber tipped thing on your gums to dispel the graininess and restore the pristine pink beauty of the tissue that will keep your pearly whites attached to the rest of you for the long haul. Oh. Translation: you take a hard metal object and press like hell into the sorest part of your mouth. *Then* you test the whole masochistic schtick with purple disclosing drops, rinse, and finally anoint the whole with *Gel Kam*, a gel fluoride, swish for a full minute, spit, then don't eat or drink anything for at least 30 minutes. I tell you, it's like a whole new religion; you must become a true believer or go bare-gummed into the void.

I did all that last night while watching *The Johnny Carson Show*. When I finished, my right arm was dislocated from swabbing my back molars, pain was shooting out from my ring finger which is osto-arthritic, and the whole ritual made me so hungry I had to grab a snack. Which dirtied up my teeth again, packed my gum pockets with food and sticky glop, and destroyed an hour's worth of excellent prophalaxis.

Therefore I say: Ask not what your gums can do for you; ask what you can do for your gums. With full apologies to President Kennedy, there is only so much I am willing to do for my danged gums, after that they're on their own.

It was 1:00a.m.—I looked at my assortment of tools, ineffectually swished a little plain water around, then said "oh the hell with it" and went guiltily to bed. As is.

I understand they're doing brilliant things with false teeth these days.

MYSTERIES

More mysteries? You tell me inquiring minds want to know? Well, here are the facts. Nothing but the facts, ma'am. Put it together as you see fit. I know I have. First clue. It is night. A very brilliant moon is out after raining hard all day in Los Angeles. The date? Thought you'd never ask. Well, it's Friday the thirteenth, the last Friday the thirteenth will be a full moon in this century. The next time this combination will occur, you will be writing 200 and something on your check stubs-check it out.

Second clue. A certain small cluttered room in the house is always very cold. Just as if it had a pipeline to the South Pole. Winds whistle in there. Breathe clouds up when humans breathe in there. If there were a mirror, would it show a reflection of anyone? Or would the glass show wisps of swirling ectoplasm?

I lay on my side of the bed in the pre-dawn hour, watching while Hubby gets ready for a long day in the office. He proceeds from his bath through the warm bedroom, and then enters his closet to get dressed. As frigid air meets tropical beads of water and clouds of steam Hubby has trailed from morning ablutions, a sort of weird drizzle ensues. This is the closet, remember, that creates its own weather patterns.

My closet and dressing area are adjacent to his, but mine stay warm and dry. Supernatural cold cloaks his padded bench, his current book, left open on the bench so he can read a little as he struggles into his clothes. *And* the man never catches cold.

My conclusion? Any sensible person would jump to the same one. Naturally I think something occult is going on in there, the equivalent perhaps, of a psychic polar bear club without the ocean. You immerse in freezing surrounds, and emerge uncannily able to weather, well, weather of any description. Not only survive freezing, non-human conditions, but to thrive, yes flourish, in air so frigid it would stun a a full-grown polar bear.

Sort of a reverse sauna bath keeping my own spouse in the pink? How does his closet cool this way when all the surrounding areas are toasty warm? Mmm, clearly a case for Thelma Moss, ghost buster to the stars.

And you think I read too many *National Enquirer*s? It is perfectly clear, my dear Watson, we have a case of Friday the 13th necromancy in house.

SUPERBOWL

Of course I knew the Super Bowl would be on this Sunday—I do, after all, have a husband and two grown sons. Actually, I look forward to it too, as a time for guaranteed peace and quiet, everybody else being plastered to the TV set. I can read, write, shop, and generally catch up. Or watch something different on another set.

What I just learned, however, has shocked me a bit—this event is to be held in L.A! I had simply assumed that football was played in more northerly, snowy places. Somehow. In fact the evening news was full of blizzards and snows extending even to Florida. Perhaps to Miami Beach itself.

It's true we had been gone, in quite dramatic cyclonic circumstances to Fiji this year, but I do know that come New Year's Day…it's football somewhere. As long as I have enough food in the refrigerator or simmering on the stovetop, exuding a message of fragrance and plenty, no more is expected of me that day. Also, having long since given up the expectation of prying anyone away from the set that day, I am no longer jealous of all that time being spent, (not on me).

I've assiduously avoided cultivating an interest in sports events on purpose. As I get older, the tube is increasingly a seduction to me. Who knew, in the youthful idealistic days of contempt for folks who watched too much boob tube, that there would be so many fabulous offerings? Although I should have realized that war bonds and jitterbug couldn't last forever as recreational fare, I never thought I'd be in danger of becoming a couch potato. Now there is cable, and equally important, there is my three-speed Barcalounger from which, feet well up, I can chuckle at Bill Cosby and *Night Court*, or adore the animal shows, or get caught up in the nuances of major issues on CNN. As there are already too many enticements, I don't want to get caught up in any sports that aren't Olympic procedures. I have a heavy study load as well, so cannot get into the sports schedule, for heavens sakes.

So, therefore, I do not know sports, although I do like their air of energy and fun, not to mention the commercials are always great during the games, so I do go into that room to say hi during them. The TV room is often jammed with guys laughing, growling or screaming with joy. So it's an interesting place to be during a big game, if only to have a close-up look of major pathology in vivo. I get to see a part of my family that emerges only as the agonies and ecstasies of narcissistic wounds and thwarted male bondings get exacerbated. These states do not bear gazing at too long, but I dare to. Am I not, after all, a matriculating member of an institute dedicated to studying human behaviour? Meaning: that's my business—studying the sane-insane continuum of our species.

So I do have plenty of work to do, not the least of which is acquiring the necessary textbooks. In fact, the assigned tomes at our school are so arcane, if you don't luck out in finding them at the Technical Book Store in Westwood, you can pretty much kiss your weekend goodbye altogether.

Because that means Biomed.

Which means U.C.L.A.

Which means it's a full-time career finding a place to park, and another one mooching through the card catalogue, replete with tricky computerized listings and huge sheets of listings published too recently to get into the regular files.

You need (once you've *become* resigned to the fact that you cannot buy, nor can you "run off" the section you need in someone else's book—yes, yes, it is illegal, I know) the legs of Tensing, the will of Nietzsche, and the eyesight of Superman to locate the volume. Your knees have to stay bent as you squat on the floor examining the bottom row of books, and your back must flex to collect and lift the various references to your little corral in the high-rise stacks. What I may be implying is that I'm about ten years too old for serious research efforts at Biomed. We do not even speak of computer search and modems here.

I did expect that if these Herculean measures were necessary, at least most normal individuals this weekend would not be competing with me for choice books in the corridors of learning, power and joint sprains.

Now, you are bearing in mind that I am just regaining control over my biorhythms after a three week jet lag, are you not? When I barely can remember to write '87 on my checks yet?

Well I'm thinking those football players are going to be up to their shoulder pads in the cold wet stuff, when suddenly I learn they are going to be here—jamming up the arteries and parking lots of our own universities. Better just give up the search for now; even a non-sports fan is affected by such huge swirls of cars and activities around such a major event. Maybe I'll watch the game, if I cannot beat them, it has been highly recommended to join'em.

WALK ON THE WILD SIDE

Not really all that wild, for a little girl from Pennsylvania used to woods, trees, nature and the occasional brown bear sharing her lunch of wild blueberries. But distinctly wilder than a walk down Melrose Boulevard transpired today when we went to see my favorite critters—the ones at the L.A. Zoo.

I've kicked caffeine, most red meats and Sweet n' Low, but my favorite addiction is one I dream about and get restless unless I can visit frequently…I just love the zoo. Have since I was a little girl and rarely got to one, there being no such thing in Williamsport, Pennsylvania.

I love the fine specimens they have, and the beautiful landscaping, the shady and sunny paths leading to old and new parts of this superior animal compound. The zoo, which I've always enjoyed, has undergone a dramatic upgrading this year. New South American areas, new areas developed make for some special sights. There is a wild cat show in a small area at the top of the main drive. Young women put baby wild cats through their paces; they turn around, jump on post, balance across a pole, rewarded for every right turn with a piece of raw meat on the end of a stick.

Some rare species like the Asian cloud leopard, a compact cat with a long tail for balancing above the trees; a jauntily striped and spotted caracel named Sneakers, and their strollers in the front row. No fence, no barbed wire nor moat protected the predator from the prey. Each very aware of the other. The babies cuddled close to their daddies, the cats waited for the moment when the leash wrapped around their keepers wrists might slip, and they looked to be ready for their chance, should it ever come.

A good selection of young representatives of the wild cat family made an appearance and did a graceful or klutzy star turn. No matter. They were patiently fed cat kibble or a bit of meat until they got it right…only affection training here. The main idea is to pitch to the public that these furs look much better on these darling felines that they would on some rich society lady. That the fur trade would not flourish if there were a boycott on killing animals for their coats. That soon a wild cat in the jungle would be non-existent, they are rare as pearls, and what a poor world a catless world would be. True.

Next, we saw elephants getting their bath, patiently turning, kneeling, and obeying the keepers as he hosed them down with clean cool water for the day. The African and the Indian elephants seemed really to enjoy this bath time, and the rapport with the keeper was obviously pleasant for both species.

Next, the South American representative, the blond and the black jaguars. Both handsome, in their prime, both with spots. The black coat showing clearly, the spots outlined beneath.

Another glamorous big cat was the solitary snow leopard, luxuriantly ensconced in the old panda bear quarters we had built for the Olympic pandas. I sure wish they could have stayed in L.A. forever. They have a lot of them starving to death in the forests of China, why couldn't these two stay here? Preposterous.

I just found out why this one gorgeous cat was alone. Yesterday, there was a picture of three brand new baby snow leopards that will be seen for the first time this coming week. Mom and kids have been cloistered up for the lying-in! Can't wait to meet them…I remember years ago when this pair were little more than babies themselves.

And the ocelots. And the woolly gibbons and all the endlessly amusing ape family…the most endearing and humanoid being the orangutans. Lounging around, trying to put leaves around their necks, and lazily swinging with one arm to their rope. Orange and furry, boy do they need protection, as their tiny rain forest home is decimated around them in Malaysia; they are just about out of living space on this planet, except for the zoos.

Other favorites, a lone spectacled bear who walks around and around in his swimming pool looking for all the world like he was doing laps or working out to a video.

Finally, the *piece de resistance* this clear breezy July day. A troupe of West African dancers performing at the main …*Jewel of the Nile.* They spin, shake, leap and wriggle, acrobats par excellence. I think of mambo dancing, when they sailed across to South America. The movements could shade into belly dancing as they inched north to Egypt. The leaps look like Olympic quality gymnastics, and there was such shaking and jumping going on! I was tempted to join them when they invited the audience to come dance with them, but if I had gotten into it, I fear it all would have ended up in the ward for the terminally sprained and stupid.

Yes sir, I am addicted to the sounds, the smells, feels and atmosphere of the place that lets us in on a reality so different from the mean streets just five miles away in downtown L.A. Our zoo is cleaner, newer and more entertaining than ever before…I say go take a walk…it's a hoot. And a roar.

LONDON PART NINE—LEARNED LESSONS

Thursday, we went through the Royal Palace and Pavilion at Brighton. Friday to Windsor. Room after room after room. Neat, vacant.

UNACCOUNTABLE

Numbers, counting, spatial relations are not my thing...unh, unh… not my bag. From the first time that I remember anything, I knew that. Call it genetic, call it environment, all I know is when they passed out ability with numbers and anything with measuring, you know, sciences with metry attached as in telemetry, geometry, optometry, I was A.W.O.L.—out to lunch, or the cosmic equivalent thereof.

I just never got it, and in spite of screams from the propagandists of recent years, do not think this connotes helplessness or unhealthy female passivity. Psychologists will sneer, and insist that I just don't *want* to count, so I won't be accountable to anyone, get it? Attitudes like this are poison to women liberationists. Gloria Steinem would fume and Betty Friedan will fuss, but I don't count, multiply, subtract or do fractions, I never have, I probably never will, and no amount of private tutoring or trying to shame me about this has made one iota of difference.

I tried to pass the non-verbal part of the G.R.E.'s one time, but I was so non-compis (thick, dull, obtuse and dense)...it was so bad I decided to go to a school that didn't require them for a clinical major. There never was hard proof before, but I never doubted that when numerical or spatial abilities were handed, I was short-changed...I have had this inner knowledge forever, that I just couldn't get it, and the only reason I'm admitting it now is I feel good about myself otherwise, to be able to be honest.

Mostly I blamed this state of affairs on Mr. Roy Quakenbush, my third grade teacher. He wore some kind of a dead black animal on his head, which he parted down its middle, and had no middle finger. Furthermore, he was some kind of manic-depressive; I know that now after a lot of study, I didn't then, of course. All I knew was he was weirder than even the run-of-the-mill weird teachers back then, and frightening. When he was up, he would dance around the classroom to some inner fandango, and when down, he growled, threatened and behaved like Attila the Hun, patience-wise. The man was morbid, needing only to sit on a doorpost quoting "nevermore" to set the stage for tragedy. I was most afraid of him when he was twirling around the room peeking looks down the little girls' blouses. Somehow he imperiled the mental health of the whole grade with impunity. I also blame my mother who was forever exhorting me not to think I was smarter than boys, and certainly not to show them if I did think I was. Smart girls did not do math, mother intoned. I guess she thought I would always have a firm of accountants at my beck and call when I grew up. So between Quackenbush's obvious nuttiness and my mother's grandiose ideas, it all eluded me. Plus, it really never made much sense after second grade...as much math as I ever want to do, I learned before then.

So, from then to now, I have limped and bluffed along. I managed so little money when I was single I could easily handle it all, and after that; oh woe is me when the militant mommas hear this, my husband has done all the toting up ever since...and he is welcome to it.

Today, in the March issue of one of the University School of Public Health wellness letters, I read that estrogen levels affect perception and spatial relationships. When they are verified to be high, women do not do as well with depth, spatial relations and *numbers*. Ha, I always knew it. Did beautiful Williamsport girls not get married, have children and live happily ever after (or at least till they moved to a community property state), and did plain ones not go into graduate school? Who wore a dead black wig on his head, parted in the middle and resembling nothing so much as a portrait of the raven who oft times quoth "nevermore" to a poverty-ridden Edgar Allen Poe? He was morbid about math, and spread a pallor or fear and depression in his third grade Williamsport classroom. In his *depressed* state. In his *manic* aspect, he ogled girls' sweaters and danced maniacally around the classroom; both states were awful, but we feared the dancing Basque the most. He could go completely off the deep end and imperil us all; we figured getting stomped to death was too high a price to pay for mastering factoring and fractions. I was afraid of him; I know it sounds like something out of Peter Pan, but he had the end of one of his fingers cut off, the whole last joint actually, and that, combined with his power and obvious zaniness, gave me an unhealthy attitude toward math which persists to this day. So, all this time, from then to now, a not inconsiderable span,

I have limped and bluffed along on my own; I didn't make enough money to get any of it mixed up. Since then I have had a husband who "took care" of anything to do with bookkeeping and numbers. When I lunched with the ladies, someone else told me how much I owed, what the tip was for us each, and I'd plunk it down. I'm not proud of this, but I just knew if they let me do it, we'd cheat, be cheated, or end up in Leavenworth. It was a shortcoming I accepted, having once paid a tutor to try to get me through the G.R.E.'s to do respectably well in the non-verbal part to go to graduate school. The tutor did poorly with me, so did the second one. My husband finally taught me 8 times 7 by jumping out from behind a door and telling me the answer. That evidently made an impression on me; to this minute I know the answer is 56. But there was a limit to the time, money and doors we were willing to spend to teach me fourth grade math, and I settled for a school that didn't need G.R.E.'s. What I wanted was a clinical program in the humanities anyway, for crying out loud, and I could hire an accountant when the time came that I needed one.

Maybe I had been brainwashed by my mother, whom I also blamed, of course, for telling me girls were not good in math. Or maybe it was the fashion when I was in grade school that we let the boys excel, and *then* I became phobic about it. At any rate I couldn't do it, and that was that.

In the past two days I have been elated to find hard research from respectable sources that actually *names* this condition, and assigns me a diagnosis, a category other than Big Dummy. Innumerate! I am to numbers what the illiterate is to letters. (Well, not entirely, I can recognize them when I see them and do some rudimentary figuring, nothing tricky, of course. No tips…yes yes, I know; there are tip cards that figure that out for you, but the print's too small to read, even with my bifocals on.)

When I am trying to sound competent, I quote figures I have read in the papers and am invariably off by hundreds, thousands, millions…I'm, profligate with other people's money.

Another piece of research which will have the feminists on the boil is that women's hormones have something to do with it, and the more estrogen, the less math sense. *I knew it!* Pretty girls don't need math, they get large handsome men to do all that for them, or buy tip cards. Oh, I know, I know, such progressive ideas are reprehensible, but that's the way it always was for me.

The bloom is off the rose these days, however. Men do not seem to be rushing up from the sidelines to add up my bills for me. The girls are slapping their American Express charge cards down with fearful assertiveness. The age of being charmingly incompetent have gone out with he power bubble bath. Men are getting manicures and permanents and having their eyelashes dyed.

Could someone print me up a small card with the times' table on it, and a breg chart with the most common subtractions? Oh, mechanical difficulties go along with this personality type, and I cannot make any number of pocket calculators work for me, nor big ones either. For that, you have to have much more of a sense of how numbers work than I do. I'm never really sure of what the signs really mean, and get those little marks at the top of the keys all mixed up, like = + % A $ # Divided by's are the worst, I've never gotten the sum right even once on my pocket calculator; I'm jinxed in that way.

COLONY

Sorry for the revanchist views, but folks, all you have to do is to look at your TV every night. Even the all no-Jay stations sneak peeks into the trial every day, at least here in L.A. they do. Leno has a hilarious skit about the trial every night on his show. And I agree with him, that it is unfortunately, the comedy event of the century. I mean, with Dan Quayle, there was a blooper every six months or so, with Jerry Ford, we had to make do with an occasional assaulted golf game bystander or a trip up the steps to an airplane every once in a while.

But with O.J. by God, it is *The Gong Show* each and every court day. There is some outlandish ploy on the part of the Desperate Defense to try to inject reasonable doubt that this oh-so-obviously-guilty man did not do the deed.

The majority of people in this state, probably in the country, feel that their precious hero must have been framed. I don't care what the facts show, they think we establishment folk are out to get this black man who clawed his way up from the projects of San Francisco. Certainly his had been a realization of the great American dream. Exactly like Elvis.

Both larger than life people, handsome, charismatic, one immensely talented in music, the other a brilliant athlete...both coming from the most profoundly dirt-poor levels of society. But O.J. is, on top of a darling public persona, a symbol to a much oppressed minority of one of their own making it. And Michael Jackson, to whom I have been mentally giving the benefit of the doubt since his alleged victims have been teen-agers and not young children or babies, has thrown in his support for this famous figure. As Jackson has wisely said, the American people want to build up all famous black people only to enjoy tearing them down.

There is nothing at all similar in the legal problems of these two popular icons. Jackson's victims were delivered to him by their venal, benighted or naive parents, and furthermore had a mouth and could have complained or told the police, or run away at any time. Nicole and Ron Goldman had no such choices about their lives. Jackson murdered no one, Jackson beat up no one.

All evidence, his history and his profile of narcissism, possibly drug induced rage and violence points to him as it. The probable perp. However his closet pal, had one bad thing to say about him.

However...he is, in a most primitive sense of the word, American royalty.

Ensconced in the psyche and soul of his fans, as deeply as the British people treasure their monarchs whether or not they misbehave. Our icons...right or wrong. Sacred symbols of a deeply held loyalty, on the level of a religious enthusiasm.

Just look at football fans. There are people who astonish me by being sanely appropriate and level headed, except when their favorite team is in peril. Then these same folks go certifiably ballistic; the team means something more than a sports event, it touches some core issues. For those who identify with a particular team or entity, its losses or failures are the same as their own. Thus the endless outpouring of support for O.J.

O.J.'s book is a best-seller; he is making tons of money from signing cards and pictures, statues, every kind of memorabilia. Eighty eight per cent of black men in this country think he is innocent, that he has been framed by the police. After all, it took Rodney King two trials to get any justice. Even the most stand up impartial jurors have black fathers, brothers, boyfriends or husbands who have likely been hassled in some racist way, and that they are going to have to go home to after the trial, how will they be received in their community if they are seen to be on the side of the pigs, not the brothers?

In spite of well-documented beatings of Nicole, which are the indicators of a vicious streak, jurors may think only of the charming sports figure and deny with all their hearts the monster behavior.

There is a need to elevate him to the untouchable level. He didn't do it, but if he did, it wasn't that bad. She was a commoner anyway, who really cares about her or Ron?

We need to adore him; we will spend untold millions on his defense, parading one after another dim-witted confused witnesses to try to reverse the mountain of evidence against him.

Even though the defense presumably screened out the most psychotic of the folks who volunteered to defend O.J. and witness for him, they are stuck with a confused, motley assortment of contenders for fame and fortune suitable for a feature part in *The Twilight Zone.*

Bring back the royals! At least we know our feelings are for irrational parental substitutes. We need to have someone in the flesh to worship here on earth, so we don't have to sublimate and put murderers in place of crowned heads, who themselves fill in for a dynasty of deities.

I predict a mistrial, a likely scenario as the sequestered jury gradually will start to decompensate in their virtual prison conditions. They have started to already, five of them. Next guess is acquittal. I think, frankly, the D.A. should be thrilled with a hung jury; at least they'll get another chance.

There will always be enough American jurors who will think their idol is blameless. Larger than life. Not subject to the same rules as everyone else.

He should have been in jail long ago for the battery he visited upon his wife, whether or not she filed a charge. He beat the system once, he'll beat it again.

But black folks say, *not this time. This* black man has the money, friends and resources to play the white man's game. He has hired the best, black and white, who know how to play (abuse) the system and this time, *we* will abuse the justice system for our Hero.

Magic Johnson...infected
Michael Jackson...suspected
Mike Tyson...rejected
O.J. Simpson...inspected.

LONDON PART TEN—WELCOMING

Oh God, the tube...even the Mayan pyramids didn't have flights of steps like that. If you're not spending World War II in one, who needs it? I no sooner rest and heal my knee, thereby wasting many precious days I could be sightseeing, but then, boom. We get out of the theatre, can't find a cab home, and are forced to take the Underground home or stand on a street corner for hours. Us jocks—we got trouble! I usually feel like Bill Walton when I have to ice and elevate my knee.

Their spectacular courage in the face of unspeakable atrocities. It is hard to forget the British and forgive the Germans even now that they are respectably bourgeois like us. The wonderful, wonderful *not boring Goring*. I feared it would be a nasty, dull, but convenient business/commercial establishment. We booked in because it is around the corner from the place where Hubby is working. A truly rare morning at home in our suite, washing some, sorting some and sending out some laundry when, very faintly, I began to hear rollicking, bagpipey sounds. Is the radio on? No. Louder and louder, the lively music fills the suite, and then horses' hooves and marching boots. A parade coming toward? No! Right past me. Literally under me, then 'round past Buckingham Palace wall...down the street come the Navy, Army, and ceremonially dressed soldiers I could never see in the vast mobs in front of Buckingham Palace on a Sunday morning. Our chambermaid was in the room at the time and I said, "What's going on?" She and I stuck our heads out of our fourth floor window, luckily with a very wide stone ledge carpeted with moss—and watched—and listened as it tootled by. Ancient ceremonial garb on the lance-carriers, horse-guards troops on foot, khaki trucks full of real non-ceremonial British soldiers with very modern weapons. Right under our noses. Loved best the caparisoned horse dancing to the four corners before he led the troops 'round the corner. I know it's dressage, from the Olympics, but it danced, turned 'round, did amazing horse terpsichordia in the middle of the street. Mothers fled across with babies in between every set of armed forces. Between the Navy and before the Army, I saw from the window Peter the doorman, flying across the street pushing a trolley-load of luggage, with a frantic tourist pulling his brown valise on its lead like a large canine toward diverted cabs in the next road, obviously flying toward a rendezvous at Heathrow or Gatwick.

Then, amidst fluttering leaves, 21 dull loud thuds. Cannons of course, we1coming Monsieur Mitterrand. The usual welcome, I gather, for heads of state. This not such a pedestrian place after all!

FRANCES TUSTIN

Screwed up the courage to call the wonderful Mrs. Frances Tustin. A dear classmate urged me to do so or I would not have her that *bold.* I characteristically wondered what in the world a famous person would want to waste her time with me for, but remembered Anne Glasser's words of encouragement—oh, she'll love it. Was going to write—wrote several notes—went back to 63 New Cavendish Road to re-read some of her book again on autism—finally in a do or die attempt to overcome what I know to be disabled part of me—phoned her Tuesday at noon. She said Wednesday was her free day. She invited me to get the 10:30 from Baker St, then straight on to Amersham and she'd pick me up at the station at 11:20. I said I'd be there. I was; she was.

This wonderful person turned out to be a chubby cherub with fluffy white hair, gorgeous white teeth in a beautiful mouth and the extraordinary fine delicate pink and white English skin.

She led me through her lilies to meet Arnold, Professor Tustin, who turned out to be an 85 year-old leprechaun, albeit a tall and lanky British one. She at 71 and he at 85, funny, giggly, brilliant, pleased to have me visit. I accepted Sanka and a bran cookie, was shown the loo, also the new kitchen was shown off.

I didn't know if she had a free hour or what, and as Arnold, formerly visiting Professor of Electrical Engineering at M.I.T., announced he was starving, I wondered if I was not keeping them from their lunch. Mrs. Tustin said we would go to Ambers and Arnold would eat soup at home since he hated to go out anywhere—as he knew where everything was at home.

Mrs. Tustin drove me to an ancient mill-house building all restored with haute couture clothing, redone millstream enclosed in glass and visible in the middle of the building—and a wonderful restaurant.

We chatted away about ourselves; at the end of lunch, I asked if she would like to drop me at the station to save a trip later. She exclaimed, "No indeed, Arnold wants you to come back!"

I heard stories about Donald Meltzer, Melanie Klein, Wilfred Bion, Anna Freud. We discussed the British hatred of most analysts and psychologists, and of some of Mrs. Tustin's triumphs.

All in all, one of the loveliest, warmest, brightest couples ever in this world. I will never forget that day.

I am now emboldened to foist myself or others at any opportunity.

Professor Tustin's eyesight has been reduced to a mere pinprick of vision in one eye. He can read only half-a-word at a time. I said to him it was sad, but it could be worse. What I meant and will tell him in a tape I will send, because reading is an immense strain, that although as handicapping as the visual loss is, there is a lively mind and lean active body. (I think, of course, of my father, two years younger than Arnold Tustin. His mind is gone; whether through his many small strokes or the profound depression he's sunk into. There is not much left to encounter in a visit: crying a lot, non-responsiveness to my verbal advances, anger. An angry, sad vegetable.)

A.T. is witty—recited half a dozen adorable limericks he has written. Lively, listening intently, smoking rapidly. Every marble there and gleaming, polished, sparkling marbles they are, too.

As I left and bid him *adieu* at his door, he said to me, "You will look after Frances in L.A.—won't you?" I assured him I would, and will I ever! She greets her special friends at Ambers with, "Hello, my lovey ducks, great lovey ducks." I could have kissed her as I left, but I didn't dare hug this famous lady. I wish I had. I've never had reason to like my middle name before. Now I do. It's Frances. Named for a kind nurse who saved my life according to "me mum" when I was a few months old, and she was sure I'd know another. And now, another bitter crisis and resurrection! Another rebirth!

So many things are forgettable—the trek Sunday through Hamstead Court, for one. I was dead tired. My legs and feet were killing me. In every one of the endless series of vast rooms, I made for the window seat to have a rest and gaze over the topiary to the Thames—mainly imagining Katherine Hepburn being led away at the end of her Christmas visit, loved and hated by her king, Peter O'Toole.

But the visit with Frances and Arnold I will cherish forever.

LONDON,PART ELEVEN—LAYERS AND ART

I go out now for a nice tromp along the embankment. The sun is out, but of course I will carry and wear my foul-weather gear. Any second it could change.

Surprise—it is steadily getting warmer and warmer. I have my luggage entirely taken up with fur-lined raincoats, boots and cashmere sweaters, and with some lightweight blouses as well. I've been fooled by October before. Three years ago, arrived in New York from L.A. on Oct. 28 with a woolen wardrobe, fearing the worst. They were running the New York Marathon as they and we tried to get from Queens to mid-Manhattan. I must say our cab wasn't even a contender. We came in a bad last, trailing the last runner. And in a tropical sweat. It climbed to 88 degrees F with humidity to match. That week in New York, I scouted round for a T-shirt or something to wear. So much for autumnal planning. I've now had etched on my brain, no matter what the destination, what the clime, or whatever time: bring something for a heat wave.

Something for a cold snap.

Layers: wear clothes in layers: the British dote on layers, blouses, pullovers, cardigans, jackets, and their signature item—a scarf. Long and slopping plaidly to the trouser cuff, or short and fuzzily wrapped 'round the throat., or huge squares pinned colorfully, dramatically 'round one coat, or melting in unnoticed with the natives having a pow-wow at Lake Titicaca, or wildly ruana-like, sufficient for trekking over an Andean pass...draped cashmere or mohair falling over one, front and back...an overall over-all look (one I favor, myself, for the same reason I love pocketbooks and scarves—to wit, sizeless, seasonless.)

I can gain or lose pounds faster than British Sterling—and still have something to wear.

Hubby observes this advice more in the breach than the reality... this advice about layering—but now in the fall, have a thin cotton blouse under anything. Started out wearing sweaters Oct. 1, ended up only in blouses Nov. 1, it warmed up dramatically in the London area. By the time we departed, leaves finally turning from gorgeous green to autumnal mellowed umbers, ambers, golds, bronzes, softly palleted, richly mulched.

You don't kick and scuff crisp leaves—you squish along or jump into tame refined piles of them. Some contrast with my memories of sharp, shocking, gasp-worthy vistas of brilliant, heart-stopping, colors of fall mountains near Williamsport, PA, where I grew up.

Day before Halloween, I braved the underground—the steps killed my sprained knee—plain flat walking not arduous—took the train direct from Victoria to Richmond Station, walked 10 minutes to Kew Gardens and through the lioned gates (15 pence admission charge). Blew around Kew for an hour, it was dark gray blustery day, not cold at all but very blustery. Winds blew leaves horizontally along...Was transported back to a Halloween night when I hurried from my front door to rendezvous with other trick or treaters a few blocks away. I felt totally alone on a dark, creaky, sighing, poltergeisty kind of evening. It probably was 6:15; Nirvanas are not too scrutable, at all, not to us mortals.

Feeling ever so much better about this journal since seeing the Max Beckman exhibit at the County Art Museum yesterday. I have been feeling terribly awkward about so much focus on me and I and my autobiography—so self-centered, narcissistic? After looking at seven or eight rooms full of colorful outpourings liberally laced with self-portraits about every sixth work, I feel so much better about my focus on myself: my feelings, my sensibilities. Maybe it's okay if one is an artist, his stuff is big, messy, some canvasses with a muddy disagreeable brownish tone. The major part of his work, more garish dreamscape, more primary process than I enjoy. I like some discipline to contain a vision, even of passion. Maybe because I have so little, myself. I don't like to go look at someone else's excesses. Mainly I disliked the fleshy gross pleasure-seeking Germans of "Cabaret" and "I am a Camera" portrayal. The dark underside exists at all times in juxtaposition with the cogent and civilized. I am uncomfortable with it all sloshed over me as I look, without—I almost said any—purifying and transcending powers of the artistic vision. Van Gogh managed to put his immense passions and his statement to the world about his feelings in a form that vibrated with color and impact, but still was within the pale of—within my pale of pleasure in the seeing.

Coarse and crude that period was—okay. The depiction of a beach scene, mounds of humanity piled on top of each other at the beach, nipples and behinds popping out of overstuffed bathing suits, okay. There has to be some contrast, more than the self-portraits, which do emanate essence, and barely-controlled, or maybe rigidly over-controlled. They are the best.

I prefer by very much indeed the dreamscapes of Kafka, the primal and eerie midnight blue skies over Rousseau's sleeping gypsy with lions and other menacing forms frozen in trance above him. There can be the suggestions of the bizarre, the violent, without doing such violence to the canvas. This is art as therapy—I've seen much better stuff by real mental patients, actually.

Restraint is important. And the transformation, too—that is art.

Of course I love Flemish painting—cool, clear, realistic—better than Rococo...Dada better than High Renaissance with a billion sugary angels.

Just downstairs in the main building, a group of netsukes embodying the best example of vision; detailed meaning, restrained yet expressive material, passion, nature, human nature, even belief systems depicted by tall, dark or pale attenuated hooded figures named *ghost*. Frog on a single lily pad, some perfectly ratty rats, surrealistic dancing horses, an old man drinking milk from the breasts of a peasant woman. Maybe that's where Henry Ford got the idea: he engaged wet nurses for himself, you know. He was into embryo-newborn theory before Neiman of Switzerland.

The tiny perfect images thrilled me. A rather abstract cat sleeping. The figurate gave off a positive aura of sleep. The rounds of head and body withdrawn into the interior of the organism, closed off yet alive. One-half inch worth of perfection via ivory.

There were camellias worked in wood, pistils and stamen ideally realized all of a piece.

It is a joy to create something. One almost hates to submit it lest the bloom he criticized off its penned petals. What happiness to share this—for someone else to feel or see what we have experienced, from the process to the product. I've not yet enjoyed that on a scale larger than two. One writes because it is good to write. If it is not shown, true it's not shared, but also one is not crushed by frost or lack of empathy.

Unspeakable treasures come and go from our museums. I enjoyed a similar trove of miniatures that were literally a treasure last month at the Getty. A traveling cache of tiny ancient Greek coins, scaled down from the once massive talent—the earliest coin of the realm according to the Haraklion Museum on Crete. The original pay were the huge double-axes of copper or (triangular?) gold. How you got these to a market or made change, I don't know. But you sure had the mighty, mighty strong…

MOTHERS OF INVENTION

I'm a newspaper reader from way on back, and though I read the funnies first, I don't skip as much of it as say, Hubby does. Seems to me he reads the sports page with intensity, glances at the headlines and the lead stories on the front page, goes to work and consults his TV guide in the evenings.

I peruse the calendar, view sections, front sections, skipping completely only business, classifieds and looking sketchily at metro. Good thing I make myself read all front page items... I'm not easily flabbergasted. I was absently speed-reading an item on page one of the View section when I did a double-take of disbelief, started the column all over again, to make sure I was not hallucinating. Titled *Mothers of Invention*, the piece dealt not with a new rock group, but with an author writing about women inventors. And how they have been horribly ignored. Until recently, it was presumed women invented only for their babies.

Then Anne L. McDonald enlightened me how Hedy Lamarr was almost ignored. Hmm, familiar name, I thought, much like the actress. Except this Hedy Lamarr was highly mechanical, and the inventor of one of the most sophisticate, unique anti-jamming device to foil Nazi radar. As Hedwig Kiesler Markey, the actress patented the device with partner George Antheil, a film score composer, and offered it to the War Department. She was stunned when her offer was declined. But not surprised when after the patent expired, Sylvania adapted the invention. Today the device speeds satellite communications around the world.

Whew, this knocks me out. It's as if I were to read, oh, by the way, did you happen to know that Elizabeth Taylor at the height of her youth and beauty, and in her spare time from being a movie star adored by the masses, took out a patent on artificial blood that she concocted in her own kitchen? She's very honorly with a blender.

Or, if in the 1940s, Ava Gardener had reproduced the prototype of an astrophysics formula which has allowed men to probe deep space. The Voyager series of journeys is based on these calculations. *Oh*? Yeah!

Or, research has showed that the real discoverer of the cold fusion theory was none other than Dolores del Rio, working her giver, I mean, this is a sensation. To me, anyway. I remember when I was 22 walking down Fifth Avenue opposite to the plaza, a gorgeous crisp November day, and noticing, about a block away, a lovely woman waking toward me in the throng, she was taller then. She stood out from the other stunning, chic woman who at that time thronged those sidewalks, not like the homeless and folks in torn up jeans, backwards baseball hats and sandals who lurk there now. Anyway, as this woman approached, I was transfixed. She glowed with beauty and color, a remarkable example of homo sapiens. Then I realized of course, it was a movie star. That figured, she was larger than life right on the sidewalk. Dark luminous eyes and hair, luscious lips and cheeks, perfect features. But most of all, her coloring and figure arrested the attention of all around her. And it was this Hedwig who said it`s easy to be glamorous, all you have to do is take off your clothes and look stupid.

No lady, brilliant mechanically you may be, but it wasn`t the lack of clothes or stupid look that I saw thirty years ago. It was a woman who burned like a halogen lamp compared to the affluent. I thought she was spectacular before I knew she was a celebrity, she was more silky and lush than her glistening sables. With reporters eyeing ordinary people for the slightest scrap or gossip about a *star*, how come no one has the scoop on looks? Where extant Hedy thinks about the piece? Now she looks where and in what circumstances she lives a reprise on her shopping charges some years ago. Speculation about whether the unpaid heroine status of this beauty contributed to her desire to take more of the world`s goods then she should. There is a story here, folks, I have not heard one word of follow up since this column book review actually.

A DIAMOND LIKE MINE

In many ways, my hubby deserves credit for my inspiration. It's the old story of a partner's weakness eliciting the other's partner's strength.

In my case, it happens that Hubby is a poor listener when it comes, say, to household matters. An attorney, he can listen for hours, utterly absorbed, as to why some bumblebee pollinator is suing some nut farmer over hive rights. But when I try to share words about the vital differences between pot rump and flank steak, or how my friend Hilda miraculously lost 55 pounds, or the problems arising from another friend's sleeping with her son's roommate, I lose him.

He'll start listening, but then the *McNeil-Lehrer News Show* captures him, or he absorbs himself sorting and opening the mail, or he kind of absentmindedly leaves the room. I confess, I'm easily put off unless someone is looking right at me when I'm speaking. In the old days, when this happened, I began a slow sizzle. So certainly, at these times, I tend to feel ignored. Although he is often adamant that that he's followed my story implicitly, I'd begun to tailor my stories to peter out just about when his attention does.

One day I resolved to grab more of his attention by using his own favorite medium in which to communicate. Instead of chatting, blabbing or dribbling, I took up scribbling—writing that is.

He adores reading almost anything I have written. I think he's amazed that I continue to produce something besides two kids and dinner, as I have for all these years. In a way he's primed to be receptive. I get an alert, attentive audience and otherwise more his attention.

It's not only an ideal solution, but the way I got started committing my thoughts to paper on a regular basis—and I can tell you it's kept our marriage out of divorce court. I get to express myself thoroughly, his peace and quiet are ensured. I finally feel heard, without uttering a word.

With my fidgety spouse, I merely did what thousands of neurolinguistic programmers recommend: Appeal to the receiver's favorite modality. Admittedly, if he's musical, you might want to compose on an instrument other than a word processor. If he's visual, you may want to take to oils or crayons. Whatever you take to, remember to take heart in the fact that we don't know what ancient couch potato may have inspired Michaelangelo, Paganini or Bach. Maybe you can turn your spousal lump of coal into a diamond, like mine. If not, zirconium, for many, often does nicely.

ARE YOU LISTENING?

A horrific battle is shaping up between the listen-to-your-body—its and the *do it* cadre.

I personally got sick and tired of all the excuses my body churned out for me—and the scaredy-cat/wimp-ette it sometimes seemed.

So I managed to accomplish quite a bit by ignoring it, as in "yes you do <u>too</u> want to go for your walk."

"You do <u>not</u> want to gobble up that fatty oily chunk of junk cake/candy/cookie that will clog you arteries and shorten your life."

"Yes you are going to show up and take that test even though you are terrified of it—because it is what you <u>said</u> you wanted to do. Remember? And you <u>can</u> do, so don't be a big baby."

Sure, it's fine for those of you who are strong and reasonably steady at the helm to say "listen to your body."

But suppose you'd got into my body instead.

What's that you say? Oh, if it were your body you never would have allowed it to get into this dilapidated condition.

Oh, right, I know. I used to say the identical thing when I witnessed my relatives kvetching all over the place. Never me—I vowed to myself.

Then what do you do when million of years of evolution and countless genetic pools merge and the little genes and chromosomes stand up to be counted?

And named.

And described.

And by God and be damned if they don't end up traitorously, whimperingly turning out to be exactly like Aunt-Sister-Mother-Father.

Try it. *Try* to defy your genetic inheritance. I double dare you.

You lose 40 pounds and 20 inches by Sheer Grit alone. You get involved in a crisis, turn your attention away for a moment or two and *zap*—its all back.

Try to struggle with the genes of ancestors who could have survived the siege of Stalingrad, plus a trip across the Mojave desert and still not tally depleted the saddle bags on their thighs.

Let me look at your parents, and *their* parents, or facsimiles thereof—and I'll tell you what you'll likely be at 50.

Statistics are statistics. If both parents are roly—count on it. You're poly.

Not yet?—Wait.

It catches up, unless you become a total maniac and never let that guard down.

Then you become Dr. X from UCLA who believes systematic under-nourishment plus 150 vitamins pills is your ultimate answer.

That's a whole career by itself, taking that many pills with one and a half grapes as food.

That is going too far for me.

It's not my fault I developed silver, frizzy hair. Not that I have ample hips.

Or an interest in whatever I'm interested in. I believe in socio-biology.

With a vengeance.

If the environment doesn't get you—your early conditioning will. "Eat it for me, baby".

Only trust family or whatever stupid beliefs you imbibed with your Gerbers. Some of my injunctions were: "And nice girls don't do math!"

THE HELL WITH NOUVELLE

Three tiny but beautiful abalone shells glitter softly in the lamplight of the hall table. Their glimpse of silver and pastel hue reminding me of the evening we acquired them. It was the last night I ever ate nouvelle cuisine. Let me tell you about that. There are four ways that dinnertime can be handled—you can stay home and stuff yourself, you can go out and stuff yourself, you can stay home and dine very frugally (that means find hardly anything to eat), or and this is by far the very worst choice of all, you can go out and starve.

That happened to us regularly as we returned Friday night after Friday night to a totally charming little boite very near our home. These were the beauties of the restaurant: The decor was pure enchantment, rustic, very country, very French—fresh pots of herbs and baskets of plants everywhere, an outdoor brick patio, totally attractive personnel (fresh and winsome) proximity, good neighborhood and street parking. But this final night they went one pea pod too far and alienated me completely! Boy what a mistake! I ordered a special of the evening, baby abalone. After all, I adored all abalone and fresh abalone, this fresh mollusk is not easy to come by if one is not an otter or a sea lion. Also the baby part usually signifies sweeter, fresher and more delectable quality (as in baby lamb instead of mutton) but the philosophy of less is more; minimalist art being more chic than say, baroque or renaissance and much less, but of the highest quality, had gone to the final outrageous denouement. There were three small shells with a mere wisp of meat clinging to the edge, four crossed slivers of zucchini, two obliquely placed peapods and a slim slash of raw, sweet red pepper rakishly hurled across the whole. I ate very, very slowly. I licked my lips. The maitre'd came over to inquire how I had enjoyed the baby abalone which he announced was a new offering on the menu. "Who knows?" I told him. I had had about one tooth-full, not enough really to make out any flavor whatsoever. I needed a whole forkful to be able to arrive at a decision like that. "How did it taste"? The vegetables had supplied the minimal daily requirement of vitamins and minerals for about eleven minutes I would say, if you were a gerbil that is. The bread and butter also were deliciously nouvelle. My meal cost $65.00. I was starving. I was furious. This nadir of nourishment marked the end of a lifestyle for us. Now we're into huge portions of blackened Cajun catfish or roast beef with six different kinds of homemade muffins on the table, my favorites being the jalapeño pepper, black molasses and banana. We love Thai food in our incredibly noisy new wave place on Melrose, where we order six dishes for four people, including incredible coconut-lime chicken stock soup. We found the best meatloaf, mashed potatoes and fresh spinach in the world at 72 Market Place. Large floppy buttered piles of food. We like a different, country French place with homemade lamb stew, four kinds of veggies, oxtail soup, and great steaming plates of wine-soaked marinated meats.

At home of course we often diet, but when out once again, we eat and damn the fashions. If I never see another infant beet or juvenile turnip in my life, let alone a midget rutabaga, it will be aces with me.

A bon vivant could not go on viving on nouvelle rations—at least he couldn't and still be the slightest bit "bon."

CHAIN LETTER

Eureka, I've got it, I've finally got it. Sometimes in life, a real answer comes along—and when it does, it feels like magic, just like magic. I've finally made up my mind. For once in my life, I'm going to go for it. I'm going to respond to a chain letter.

I've hesitated before, but what has it gotten me? Nothing. Where has it gotten me? Nowhere. I now have a credible explanation for why the left side of my hair will never curl down nicely like the right side and the back. Why I never win that vacation hideaway for two or at the very least, a Buick. Why I have been unable to lose those last few pounds left over from the holidays (the holidays in question being V - E Day, to be honest). Why? Because, until now, I'd never responded to a chain letter.

You see, I've always been angry at the chain letters that have come around oh, say once or twice a year. Just shined them right on, mostly because I got ticked off about being promised the goodies and wished the luck, while observing that an ugly threat or personality lurked just beneath the smiling surface of the epistological bonhomie.

If you continue to send copies of this letter, plus a dollar, to 50 of your closest friends, all manner of manna will come your way. Then the individuals, plus their case histories of being poor friendless slobs, are painstakingly spelled out. Money rains from the heavens, checks fall into their mailboxes, and gorgeous blondes drop into their laps.

Unless, of course, they choose to be hardnosed skeptics, in which case their nose will fall off. As I say, in the past when one of these missives would arrive-seemingly punctuated and composed by one of the worst hicks from the hills—I would sneer at it and/or discard it. But now, wow. I'm so excited; I'm not even holding my breath.

PAINT AS PROPHECY

It's come to my attention that I've imperceptibly turned into a curmudgeon, at least in the area of art. But a very special kind of curmudgeon, with distinct limits and parameters.

It has to do with modern art, lots of which has been bought to furnish a new suite for my husband's law firm.

And it has to do with quantity.

I can drive past a new house in Brentwood in the evening, and gaze through the open shutters at an all-white room: white walls, white carpet, white furniture, with one piece of pastel-squared painting over the couch, and just love it. Frequently I wish for a similarly cool, quiet room with the many-hued but serene statement dominating the opulent hush.

My house is crammed with English furniture, on every surface of which is a collection of shells or books or memorabilia of past events. I'd often like to trade it all in for a meaningless expanse of pure pale texture.

One piece of abstract art is one thing; a museum full of lines circles and blobs another. My reaction recently when visiting MOCA was not much more than bland, a fast walk-through while noting the admirable wood floors and excellent brilliant content. Seeing so many painting depicting no figure, no face, no form acts as a deadener to me; I simply do not relate to a collection of paint and canvas devoid of anything identifiable. I know the idea is to reduce art to its essentials; certainly one needn't have excess of any sort, nor tradition, "school" nor subject. But these vast canvases were empty, void and nil. One as the focal point of a room, yes. As décor. Or accent. Yes. But massed within one collection, no. All connection with common experience, uncommon experience, or life itself seems severed. A gang of wall paper samples would have more oomph.

When I think of my personal history of looking at painting, I remember being excited by the distortion of reality, the torquing of perspective in Picasso, Leger, and Braque. This fascinated me in my 20's, when I had access to collections in New York City as a student at Columbia, thrilled to be released from the bucolic pleasures of Williamsport and Penn State, where I read and read but had little access to the plastic arts. Suddenly the impressionist captured me, dazzling Seurat and, I loved them both. The riches of the Metropolitan were literally mine; I took a job on the publications staff and while measuring type and space for the labels on the Arms and Armour Collection (my job), I took many a detour through the galleries, and into the storage rooms on a lower, staff-only floor. There were paintings, pottery, mummy cases, Egyptiana, incredible treasures that were either being catalogued or waiting for a turn to be rotated with other exhibits. What a thrill to be in the rooms with no other persons competing for space around a precious object. I felt I owned it, and breathed with an owner's trembling rapture at "my" find.

Sometimes early on a Tuesday morning, before the Museum opened to visitors, I would walk into the Greek Gallery, my heels clicking on the solitary marble floor. Then it was that it all came alive for me, the silence restoring, alive now, not a dead thing for the past; that no herds of school children and busloads of senior citizens diluted the ancient energy, so fragile and easily dissipated. The breathing of the person standing beside me is enough to destroy the ambiance; I am overly aware of that too-near breath, the scarf, the kind of nose, the kind of scent of my neighbor. Alone, the object springs to life. The feel of awe comes flooding into me, the artistic awe I search for, and which I can no longer feel if talk and alien conversation, giggles, whispers intervene. My tolerance for crowded museums has disappeared since those days when my $55.00 a week salary conferred untold wealth on me.

Later on, after I married a young law school graduate who was then instantly drafted into the army and eventually sent to Germany, I got a chance to tour the great collections of Europe. It seemed clear to me, when viewing paintings such as the Guernica and Raft of Medusa, that the artist was trying to master great events in his life or an imaginal experience through painting. It was an attempt to transform raw emotion into art.

The collections of high renaissance paintings we explored in a trip to Italy, the infants, the Madonnas, the ranked cherubim and seraphim delighted, but ended up surfeiting us. We became wearied and jaded by the reds and golds, the search through heaven for meaning.

We welcomed the Flemish and Dutch schools next. Their look at the ordinary—an apple, a girl getting dressed or sitting in an open window, were like a slab of aloe on a blistered, overheated artistic sensibility. We lowered our gaze to a warm loaf of bread on a cool tiled kitchen table. Here was worldly, human behavior, and it was enough.

After we returned to this country, my passion was for new vistas on old sights, a novel way of depicting ordinary human events seemed extraordinary enough to me. Any fresh, real view captivated.

Now in the late 80's, it seems that nothing will cool the over-entertained but two-dimensional canvases devoid of essence. Have our fuses overloaded on relationships and significance to the degree that nothing will do but a work of art shall signify absolutely nothing but raw material? Apparently so. What with microchips, computer software and home shopping channels on TV. Everyone has seen all they want to see of consumables. The mind thirsts not for meaning and connection, but to break all connection and be free, quiet for a while. Maybe life has gotten too tough. The myriad of choices and freedoms has finally overwhelmed us; to rest is our only remaining need. And that modern art does supply. We need not process, explain or free associate; neither must we yearn to replicate another time or place. We have more meaning than we can handle already, the bookstores bulge with those trying with great effort to explain it all.

We no longer need look to the heavens, nor even to other human beings, for inspiration. Now we look to machines, the ultimate contrast with our soft, curved and degradable selves. Squares, right angles, colors that bleep, squeak, veer, highlight masses of shape or color stand on their own. We look to the next stage foretold by Bradbury, Heinlein, Asimov, and Clark. Tomorrow may be uncomfortable for fogies like me, but I think space and synergy with machines inevitable. Sentiment is out, matte and machines are in.

I'll try to co-exist.

MODERN MORES

I'm happy to say that I caught the second airing of the MTV awards—KCET, the PBS affiliate, kindly re-aired the special. I hate missing a big media event like this; it was a cultural phenomenon. And a truly terrifying insight into young people today—their loves, their hates, their taste. What makes them tick.

Maybe Dr. Spock and his generation of raise-em-by-the-book babies was a bust, maybe far, far more permissiveness was needed than even that gray eminence advised. Here's why. If that lot was not the most rebellious bunch of humanoids I have ever seen. Their clothes give new meaning to "way far out." Now, it's true that every generation thinks its young people are more depraved, disobedient and sacrilegious than any other. *And maybe they're right.*

Everyone from Euripedes, a Greek playwright of the fifth century before Christ, for heaven's sake, to sages of the Muslim and Buddhist worlds, have exhorted young people to follow the moral course and not to give their elders tsouris. But honestly, even Victorian rakes, among the most degenerate of folks, at least dressed beautifully, in fact were dandies. Even by the standards of other people. (Of course, these MTV'ers spend untold time and money looking raunchy, perhaps they are appreciate by their peers.)

Caligula's court didn't really specialize in wholesome, but they at least pressed their togas and combed up their hair. Jewels and snazzy scents, foods and cosmetic emollients were not unknown to the ancients.

Sartorially speaking, these TV doings (shall we call them don'tings?) were a disaster, belonging right up there on the wall of Naked Gun 2 and ½…remember where they pictured the Titanic sinking, the Hindenburg falling…Michael Dukakis?

Did entertainers ever before get onstage wearing stripes, plaids and polka dots all in one outfit? And shredded pants. My younger son looked like that going out the door to nursery school and kindergarten. In addition, his buttons were often misbuttoned. Did I scold and rail? No, I let him be, figuring his peer group would clue him about threads they liked and those they didn't. It did, now he is the second most fastidious dresser in the family, could give Ivy League lessons to Brooks Brother salesmen.

I figure the gang on MTV must have either come from the Baptist Belt or fresh over the wall of the convent, to be so raring to break any and all taboos. Or they had relatives like Huckleberry Finn's darling, but strict Aunt Emily, who fussed for hours at any infraction of etiquette.

Those small screen idols are by far the most, embarrassing group. Did you catch Prince's er…contribution? There's no rebuttal like his rebuttal…clothes courtesy Sodom and Gomorrah? Oh that's right, good taste is *out*. The ambiance was generally degenerate, I'm afraid we're bringing a new wave of fundamentalism down upon ourselves wily-nilly. I'm sort of surprised the mullahs and Ayatollahs and our good Brother Yusuf (formerly the ultra-cool Cat Stevens) have not put a price on the head of the producers, directors and cast of this shindig.

AUSTRALIA AND OTHER IMPRESSIONS

There are going to be two Thursdays in this week—the very first one of 1986. Yep, that's right. We get an extra Thursday—the catch is "one time only". One to a customer. I'm going to be so rested by work time Monday morning.

We are, of course, flying Qantas home from Sydney. This is as it should be, as I have just finished briefly patting Pumpkin, the koala who stars in the Qantas ads. But we were not allowed to pick him up—the Scots nanny–keeper said he gets too "stressed". She delivered a wee-lecture, cautioned, advised and admonished us, the visitors, firmly but kindly to "let Pumpkin walk around the ledge freely—pat only his back gently. Have a lovely pat, and then kindly let others have a chance."

She was decked out smartly in an Aussie uniform, like nothing so much as a down-under Mary Poppins, as she woke up her charge a cheery "right, there, darling, time to get up a have a look about." She tickled and scratched the sound asleep Pumpkin who opened an eye, recognized her nanny and looked a little bit interested. Nanny then popped a straw cone on its head—so that's how they get them down from trees!

She scampered by on a broad railing—I patted very, very thick fur. Very much like the sheep I petted at the Bakersfield Fair, Hactually. My heart was black and heavy. My last one and a half hours in Australia, before catching our flight to L.A.—possibly my last time in Australia. I had waited too long to have my picture taken with a "bear"!

Many parks promise you can hold one koala and have your picture taken—I was counting on this. Not here.

I returned to our car and told Dennis, our driver, my heart was broken. It was, too.

(Oops, time out—we've only just boarded, but lunch is here. Airlines, not only the big famous ones like Qantas—which, by the way, is the only "Q" word I know without a subsequent u—but even little tiny funny ones—Sun-State (Queensland Air), Garuda—ones of any size know what to do when passengers board. And that is—quick, first aid for jangled nerves! Food! Drink! Nature's first remedy. The most immediate, the most primitive comfort for any human. Back to basics, I mean *atavistic*. Work the mouth. When in doubt, distress or worse, ingest calories! Never fails. A busy oral cavity makes for a happy flyer.)

Back to our last hour. I showed Dennis the cab driver a flyer that promised to let you hold one bear. He called around on the car phone—we dashed over to the another park, rousted the koala lady from her lunch. I waited, heart in mouth, would she come out before our plane took off?

A plump young lady emerged from the small staff lunch room carrying a Polaroid Camera and what looked to be some small stuffed bears from the gift counter. I was half-right. One was a toy bear; on top of which was perched a much smaller live koala, named Tommy. The better toys in the gift shop were much larger than he was.

She handed the double-bear bundle to me, apologizing for his being wet. "He's just been sprayed." Right. This was really it. I got handed a pillow-feeling stuffed koala bear with a real live, faintly trembling tiny baby on the top. I hugged him close—he shot a glance at me through tiny bright eyes. We posed for a Polaroid snap. He started moving his head around, lightly smelling my white tank top. Now comes the crunch. And the indisputable fact that, adorable as this creature was—Miss Prissy Koala-Nanny's words rang in my ears, "You can't pick them up because they are not bright." They bite! They have claws that can rip off the flesh to the bone, if they wish. Plus, there is currently a V.D. epidemic amongst koalas (!?). Also a conjunctivitis epidemic (that explains Toronga Zoo's pink-eyed bears). Also, they are losing koala bears to diarrhea! Tommy's rear was not immaculate. I wished he was wearing a diaper. I was afraid he would think he was being bear-napped by a crazy American and bite me. I was afraid of his claws.

In short, once again, as it was proven to me that although I love animals in the abstract and at a flea hop's distance, I am afraid of them up close. I was also afraid he'd fall off the pillow-bear. That was groundless—after our intimate encounter, his keeper laughed and turned the toy bear-mattress upside down. Tommy was unfazed—he tensed his claws a tad and never blanched a whisker.

Now I've got four Polaroids in my wallet of me, Tommy and one of Hubby too. I wouldn't trade them for my new green and blue Boulder opal!

I've met—or rather found—the great Davuey of the mammal world. This huge rare shell has been unsuccessfully sought by Captain Hubby Ahab for a number of years—he searches for shells, I go for bears. The great Davuey is the Fijian term for the great triton trumpet shell Hubby has been seeking dementedly throughout the seven seas. Without luck, so far, except for glimpse at the bottom of a trough off the Virgins. Couldn't have taken it home anyway, it's a protected environment.

I've been washing my hands in the plane's bathroom ever since boarding, I think Tommy also suffered from fleas. My dermatologist is never going to believe this one—koala bear—it is. Thank God I've realized my dream of cuddling one and equally thank God it's over with.

Interesting facts: Koalas are born the size and shape of a cashew nut. They blindly creep through their mother's anatomy—out of the birth canal into the pouch. If they fall out, they are not retrieved. They attach to one of two nipples in the pouch for six months, and then are carried atop Mom for another six. That is why Tommy found his outing so familiar, and, if it dare be said, so bearable.

OPPOSITES

How H. and I ever got together—let alone stay together—is, frankly speaking, beyond me! We have different tastes in practically everything but the major ones—each other, kids, home.

In literature, we both love it—but not the same kinds. Chances are if I hate it, he'll love it and vice-versa, including this little contribution to the arts.

He loves spectator sports—and I don't. Ditto playing basketball, bridge, shell collecting and detective stories.

I love things having to do with relationships, children, dogs, cats and Erica Jong. He doesn't. Ditto long talks on the phone with friends, gossip—which of course as an analyst-in-training, I am trying to exorcise from my repertoire of behavior.

I used to love dancing but I haven't done it in so long, my glass slippers have turned into Dr. Hisses and need built-in arch supports! And, my lumbago has lumbered its last bago years and years ago.

We have, mutually, to raise our heads to see each other clearly through our his-and-hers bifocals.

And, I've slipped from a "Miss Bonwit" many long blocks downtown to "Miss Lane Bryant Chubettes" before settling at, frankly, "Matrons and/or Mother".

I like sitcoms about families—he doesn't. He doesn't even like Bill Cosby! I also like lectures about Freud, object relations and the death instinct. He would rather get on a bus to Cucamonga or go to the dentist for a week.

I love gardens, pet shows and open houses; he likes war movies and anything with Nazis in it. I love shopping malls and new department stores; infants of every description, plus their little outfits and accoutrements; he's bored "till they can throw a basketball back."

But Thank God—we both love the beach, Fiji and our kids. And, each other. What more do you want from a fifties marriage that has survived 'til the eighties?!

He loves puzzles, logic games and legal principles. Ditto eggplant parmesan. I hate puzzles, can't do any of these things—and the eggplant dish for which he is famous all over the west side gives me the pip.

I adore kittens, Elizabeth Taylor and doctor shows. All of which make him sneeze a lot.

(Do you think this match was made in heaven?)

Ditto shopping for clothes, looking at jewelry, and trying on new lipsticks.

Worst of all, he's retiring for the night with a mystery story or shoot-em-up while I am just getting ready to concentrate on some studying or writing. The man has never made it to *Hill Street Blues*, let alone *Johnny Carson.*

I'm good 'til 1:30 or 2:00 a.m. Needless to say, we do not interface at breakfast. (My face is still on my pillow.)

Fortunately, we are equally allergic to some relatives, staying with people in their homes, and camping. And we love our children, tropical islands, and many other things, but most of all—each other.

ALL MY CRASHES

Are you expecting to hear about another daytime soap opera like *All My Children*, All My Sons...something like that? No, it's not going to be like that.

Ever since Alice Kahn has decided to let her hair down on many personal subjects such as boyfriends, first gropes, first kisses, etc., I am inspired to let down my own locks about my automotive escapades. It suddenly occurred to me this morning, as I was negotiating the spiral on ramp of the Beverly Center, that the sight of every fender-bender I've been involved in my twenty-five thrilling years as an L.A. Lady, were incurred in the parking structure of a Shopping Center.

I was on my way to returning my Finally Free appliance to Brookstone; an emporium found only in the Beverly Center, which sells things you never would have thought up in a million years and never thought needed, you decided you need. (Here comes the risqué, intimate part.) One thing women *do;* but tell neither their boyfriends, husbands, or girlfriends, is to *shave* certain parts of their bodies. Although, it is generally accepted that underarms and legs should or could be shaven, most of us would rather be traded for Sheik Abdel Karim Obeid of South Lebanon than to admit that we are forced to take care of particular and sensitive places *other* than the above. I myself have been struggling with some furtive fuzz on my upper lip since roughly eighth grade. Since we do not live in a Mediterranean milieu where this is the norm, I have felt self-conscious about this hirsute happening and have sought remedy in chemicals, hot wax, and cold electrolysis to eradicate the pesky down. To no avail.

At Brookstone's, amidst the electric tongue-cleaners, the digital duck caller and heated sweater-hangers, I happened on this machine that is supposed to permanently cauterize the follicles so that they never produce another unsightly stalk of Keratin to plague the fastidious. In my lifetime!

And sure enough, the little sucker seemed to work for a while. That is, you held the pincers squeezed shut around the hair shaft for 30 seconds, and then the hair would slide painlessly out of its little follicle in your face. This happy condition continued for six months or so, but suddenly the magic disappeared. That is, the hair no longer *slid*, even though the little red light came on, indicating that the radio waves were operational. Now it was exactly like plucking out hairs with an old, stone-age tweezers, it hurts and left an angry red bump on your face. Clearly out of order. True, when I put a tuft into the vise, the TV hissed and sputtered, and the TV picture went seriously on the blink, just exactly as it did when it was working smoothly to rid my otherwise perfect self (?) of this imperfection, nevertheless the special, space age energy that made it all hop to, head up and left.

That's why I was forgetfully traversing the congested La Cienega entryway to this mecca for the bored and upscale. I had completely forgotten my abstinence pledge; no shopping centers unless I left the car with the valet parking, then let all the dents and mishaps be upon their heads.

I am facing into my 40th high school reunion in Williamsport, PA., next weekend. My mind wanders back to Latin. To Miss Stout; to Bill Conrad, who sat in front of me, was on the football team, good-looking, and a perfect brute. That is, he teased, sneered and made comments about my furry upper lip. The thought of facing him again without solving this problem hastened my drive to exchange or get my money back for the promised gimmick that did not provide the promised relief. Thoughts of further humiliation speeded me up the ramp, to precisely the spot where a certain 18 year old Jose from Mexico had side-swiped my car just four months ago. He was very sorry. He did not speak English.

He had no insurance, no driver's license and was terrified. I understood that this was his cousin's van, so he backed up into me instead of braving the overhang.

I did not call the police. I did not call my insurance. I did not kill Jose. It was all hopeless, I just let him go after giving him a good multilingual scolding, and had my car fixed. The insurance jump would have been more punishing.

The first new car we ever had in L.A., a forest green ford LTD, I banged into a post in Bullock's parking lot. Last week, Hubby smacked a lady driving a week-old white Olds as we were leaving the west side Pavilion. She cried. He reported. We paid.

My exchanged appliance is working beautifully again. I am becoming hairless as a Chihuahua. I may face Bill and ask him "Quo vadis, *Billius Bullies?*"…when I see him.

VOODOO

It is a very large closet. And, like other large geographical entities, it seems to attract its own climate and environment.

Recently, times have been quite dramatic in my husband's closet. Who says we don't have seasons in Los Angeles?

There is a monsoon condition prevailing in his closet right at this very moment. Nowhere else in the house, mind you. Just there. There was a pelting rainstorm last night; our sump pump evidently *did not*, so *the closet* got activated by mega amounts of water.

There is so much water in the bottom of his closet, there are actually small waves, and *yes*, can it be tiny riptide! I feel rapport with the people living on the Great Lakes! Fortunately, not too many old shoes and brown paper bags full of mismatched socks and nine-inch wide ties have to be evacuated, because of the total purge just two weeks ago as a result of a ferocious and totally local moth attack. All Hubby's good socks and sweaters from Harrods were attacked and killed by closet moths, which flew out of the closet in beige billions, leaving their zillions of eggs behind. These must be London moths, who like Turkish delight for dessert.

No other closet in the house had moths. It is spooky. Like *Amityville Horror*, only shrunk down to six-feet by five-feet of space.

I've never heard of just one part of a house being so jinxed.

Whatever is spooking Hubby's clothing environment, thank heavens; I've missed the curse this time around. Voo Doo!

PET ROCK OR SILVER LININGS?

There is a rock in our garden which contains the keys to our house. I only hope the local crooks do not read the same catalogues I get telling how all this works. Attention: all prospective robbers—I am only kidding. Our house is heavily armed and secure, plus there is nothing much worth stealing inside anyway. It's already been stolen. Okay? All set.

Right, well, in the rock garden behind our house, there is one rock which is fake; it has a little false bottom. Only I know which one it is, you will never find it, so forget it. You will never find it in a million years, and if you do, you will be sorry because I have the area in front of it booby-trapped. That's right, I saw movies about the Vietnam War, and I learned about attractive nuisances...you know, you pick it up, and it blows your legs off.

This plan evolved upon returning from an arduous trip to the Bahamas. The second island we visited, after Nassau, was Eleuthera, and the airline and airport left a great deal to be desired, modernization-wise.

We were trying to return to L.A., after a very interesting respite in these green little islands, and the Bahamas Airplane was five hours late, par for the course, unfortunately, the wait took place in an outdoor structure a-buzz with mosquitoes as big as Piper Cubs. I was bitten so many times between twilight and takeoff, it was a distinct possibility there would be little of me left to board the plane when and if I ever got there.

What to do? Our house was secured to a fare-thee-well, smug and impenetrable, trick window we always used to jimmy open, like in situations had been sealed fast shut a burglary ago. After two or three prowls around the house, we congratulated each other on what a good job of burglar-proofing we really had done. What a safe house! Then we sat down on our suitcases and thought. We though, we itched, and we examined our blisters.

Our options were to walk to a phone and call our security company, to go to the nearby hotel and check in for the night...that seemed the fastest way to get under a cool shower or just break in.

We both said, oh what the hell and ran around the kitchen. Hubby pulled out all the screens and lifted them away, the alarms screamed, sirens howled, bells rang...Hubby removed the glass louvers and everything but missiles coming out of their silos went off. Planes began scrambling in North Dakota and pilots zipped up their jumpsuits off the Bering straits. I thought we were at war. I ran around the front again to make sure no one stole our suitcases off the front-stoop before the police arrived. Meanwhile, Hubby climbed a patio chair and hoisted his paunch over the sill, falling head first into the stainless steel sink.

I scanned streets to welcome and reassure the security people, the cops, or the Psychiatric Emergency Team, whichever showed up first. Who was defending west Los Angeles tonight I wondered? Meanwhile, Hubby dragged his shoelaces out of the garbage disposal, and looking a bit tense and slightly buttered...someone had left the sink greasy...came through the house, triumphantly opening the front door for his lady in waiting. Bruised but proud, he turned off the alarm and kissed me hello. The phone had been ringing and ringing...I grabbed it. The security people were making their phone check; they aren't stupid—although there is lots of crime, 99% of the time the alarm is set off by the homeowner himself. The panic set in when they asked me for certain secret codes and other information; I had been traveling too long and forgot them all. Who can remember his grandmother's maiden name at a time like this? The doorbell rang, lo and behold, it was L.A.'s finest. At the critical second, I remembered the codes, maiden name, and favorite figurines in history, identified ourselves to the police (who wrote up a false alarm ticket and were not amused by our escapade), and ordered the screens and windows to be prepared in the morning... we'd take our chances through the night, or what little was left of it.

We went to sleep in our very own fresh bed, feeling like the stars of a Pee-Wee Herman movie, or at the very least Boy Scout Eagle Scout patches.

Once was enough, however. We've devised new intricate plans for this emergency, including the pet rock. But, as I say, don't feel challenged, any of you with anti-social tendencies, please. It won't be worth your while; we have some new trick systems to defeat any prowlers. I am now doing my Christmas shopping in F.B.I. and C.I.A catalogues and I can only tell you James Bond doesn't have a thing on me. Hubby and I are eating fish and oranges to increase our brainpower so we can remember to take our keys, and if we don't, to remember how all our new hi-tech junk works for the moment. I have certain codes, rocks, plants, and bear traps firmly in mind; Hubby's lost his paunch, in case he has to clamber over the sill again, and I've been motivated to work out to keep lots of oxygen coursing through the little Gray cells. See? About silver linings? We found ours.

SNOWFLAKES

Is there some celestial cosmologist who can tell me why scientists have emphatically decreed "No snowflake is precisely like another"? How can the weather God put his unique imprimatur on every single bit of cold fluff that melts on my cheek in a mere nanosecond? With its provenance intact and clearly recorded? Why this incredible miracle for some inorganic stuff, each flake has six sides and is a crystal. As it drifts to earth and becomes slush. Or ice. Or mud. Or hail. Or fog. Or mist. And runs through my flowerpots to feed their roots. Just think about turning a frozen smile on someone's face into tears. With just a fractal of a degree of warmth. I.e. — If it's above 32% Fahrenheit, its frozen no longer—just wet stuff-water tears. Also, what evolutionary advantage would constantly changing shapes confer? Life forms change for good reasons. Must snow flakes evolve to pursue prey more swiftly?

Ice ages have alternated with warm steamy ones for eons past. You are telling me that there is evidence to accurately infer no ancient or modern flake is exactly like another? Not even on the Kamchatka Peninsula (filled with grizzlies) who occasionally eat tourists or Copenhagen filled with tourists who occasionally eat Danish pastries?

The odds against two Identical snowflakes are awesome. But somebody does win the lottery every week. Not twin sacred flakes from The Dalai Lama's Palace in Tibet. Unlikely, in the randomness of the universe, show me more evidence! Or else, case closed. Jurors dismissed.

BAMBOOZLED

I have a problem. You may be able to grow the supposedly easy stuff in your garden, but I can't. Thriving geranium and nasturtium should be a given here in west Lost Angeles. In my garden, they are a taken. Don't ask me why. Salinity, acidity, porosity, morosity…what afflicts my common, even pest plants is a mystery. (Other malevolent conditions such as solidity, morbidity, fluidity, stupidity, rabbitity might be imagined in this context as well.)

Neither morning glory nor honeysuckle takes over my yard. In my opinion, their Donald Trump-like reputation for pushy is highly exaggerated; I can't even get them to bloom, let alone spread.

The only item actually living up to its billing as being easy grow is the running gold bamboo. Some nincompoop of a landscape gardener I hired for ecumenical reasons six years ago planted it, and we are now fighting to keep it from swallowing up Brentwood.

The damn stuff is staging guerrilla warfare. While alarmed neighbors watch for it to sprout up on one side, it is circling around and sneaking in the opposite end. A thick brown stalk appears, far from the mother plant. In a day or so, it's a foot high, sporting a tuft of tiny green leaves on its crown.

By the third day, it has leapt up another foot and broken out of the paper-like sheath to reveal itself without protective camouflage… as a bright green stalk of the dreaded bamboo. I use my jungle knife to hack it.

Down before it expands and toughens into an unbreakable, uncuttable organism.

The fourth day, 12 relentless brown stubs break ground. Never mind the individual; all that matters to this fanatical plant is the species and eventually victory.

I have investigated taking out a contract, as it were, on the mother. "Will digging out stop the spread?" I queried hopefully. "No. Nope. Negative and *nyet.* Nothing will ensure you have gotten it. It's like cancer that has spread. Metastasized bamboo is what you've got; it runs for twenty feet beyond and under your property. Even if razed, beheaded, drawn, quartered and boiled in oil, the root system will continue to fling out extensions of itself."

Great…my own doomsday machine, just what I always wanted: a mindless, eternally spreading entity. I've thought of several desperate measures, but then I am a desperate homeowner:

A. Move. To an area far from the spreading root. Maybe Newark.

B. Agent Orange. Defoliate the whole place.

C. Harvest and supply all of McGuire's furniture needs. Elegant rattan lounge ware costs a fortune; eliminate their Philippine connection; we'd be the local supplier.

D. Convert this lowly plant into haute cuisine, rather like the upgrading of the pesky snail into escargot…voila! A delicious, profitable transaction. Introduce "hearts of bamboo" to Wolfgang Puck as the natural successor to baby beet or infant turnip. Could be trendy.

There has to be some redeeming quality to this stuff, and by God, I am going to find it. Does it not provide cover to many worthy democracy-loving but harassed peoples, fleeing the tyrants of Southeast Asia? Might it not be the stuff of fables for our children: here resides tenacity in all its primitive persistence?

Why not Pandaid? There's been Band-aid, Farm-aid, and AIDS-aid. Should Panda bears alone be deprived of their chosen nutrition? We could bundle the little shoots up and ship them to the hungry raccoon relatives in the Chinese forest. From there, who knows, we might lure some of them over here to graze.

Okay, for now how about a truce in honor of the cunning non-bear Panda bear? May he be the final winner in this 1,000-year War of the Greens.

AMADEUS

So Amadeus was a boor at court.

By today's standards, he might even have been considered somewhat in. Think of *Animal House*. Think of *Dynasty*. Now there is a ditsy show. Relations coming and going, sisters, sons, daughters all showing how really crazy people are (having always been, actually), but well covered up and packaged by the church or court to "look good." there always were crudities, affairs, young girls chased under tables: Lolita, Mary Worth. Now, I've followed Mary Worth, and all the comics for that matter, for 25 years. There's always been a storyline no matter how protracted. That eventually dissolves into something like a solution. At least an ending. Then a new tenant moves into the complex where she is the resident den mother and *yenta cum laude* with gentile nagging privileges.

Now—no more. The characters never are out of trouble. Nothing is ever resolved, just new stories mixed in with the old fermenting are out of trouble. And it goes on. And on. And on. Something like life.

Martha Dare never can decide between Keith and her rich beau. Now her son, Kenny, gets kidnapped just as the wicked sister of Burt is due to return to London. I have been waiting, in my morning reading of the comics, which I turn to seconds after perusing the weather blurb on the bottom of page one, since returning to L.A. from Europe in November.

Nada, this signifies a departure from good comic protocol. I haven't watched the soaps since Dane was slurping his infant peas and carrots in his baby seat on the kitchen table, and I got hooked on *As the World Turns* for a couple of years. You could tune back in every couple of years, as I did, and recognize all the same folks, generally going over all the same old stuff.

Life has sped up. Fresh complications are expected periodically if one wants to be *au courant*—or at least with it.

So, oddities, fetishes, hang-ups, anomalies are the order of the day. Dustin Hoffman is a leading man. Cindy Lauper, not Myrna Loy, reigns on the marquee. Freaky is in.

Amadeus would be happily pledged at any fraternity on Gayley Drive this week. Wolfy was simply a young punk, ahead of the craze for punk dress that soars today in the firmament of fashion fad.

PEOPLE AND PERSONALITY

Greek vs. English! Oh what a contrast! In Greece, as one steps into a taxicab, the driver turns all the way around to scan your face, inquire about you, where you want to go, usually where you are from, and to offer, with a warm smile, his pack of cigarettes to you. (The Turks have occupied Greece for so long, I think every man, woman, and child smokes continuously.) I almost choked to death on smoke, even in the allegedly non-smoking section of the planes of Olympia Airlines. I finally carried a translation into Greek of "No Smoking Please" with me and flashed it at people with an ingratiating smile.

In London, the cab drivers seem to be half a mile away in the front, asking "where to" without turning around and with a sliding glass window between you into the bargain. British and Americans often barely understand one another as is—and the exchange in the cab trickles faintly back and forth through the open crack in the "privacy shield."

London cabbies are not talkative and must be very unhappy behind their transparent glass screen to protect the cabbies. Greek cabbies breathe garlic happily into your face—and, on passing through their own neighborhoods, stop you in to meet their mother, wife and babies. Our driver, Nick, did this in Athens. His young wife produced some Coca Cola, sweet bread with raisins, and two darling girls, 22 and 8 months old. She also dashed to her dish cupboard and produced a little gold-plated apple with almonds inside and a medal on a ribbon attached to the stem bearing the name of the saint for whom the baby Stella was named.

FINALLY AND FIRST

Traveling through time warps like Captain Kirk and Dr. Spock, undergoing bizarre artic spells in Waikiki and serial breakfasts—actually serial cereals—on route to the Southern Hemisphere, keeping one sharp eye out for sharks and the other for Halley's Comet, is it any wonder I qualify for day care? Occupational therapy? A half-way house for those of us with one part of my brain hurtling toward one hemisphere and the other hemisphere lolling behind? Not beamed up yet. Stuck in the past. The real past—past L.A., N.Y.C., Washington D.C., San Francisco, Williamsport, PA., Philadelphia. *That past* and *past that.*

Odessa. Before that, maybe—Athens, Delphi, Knossos, Koz, Illyria, and Hellespont.

(A green-yellow toad the size of the Arizona just hoped off the grass. I'm gonna lock the screens tonight!)

BIG IS BEAUTIFUL

I stay away from these. Clothes are cheap, attitudes defensively strident. In "Larger Fittings," attitudes, hopes, and fabrics are richly subtle and aristocratic. No need to scream and show off. A lady is a lady, and no one gets rude or bossy toward a few extra pounds.

EPIPHANIES

(Or, The Reason for the High-Falutin Title to This Tome)

On the personal side, I had quite a cathartic experience in the zoo, which is the reason for all the encomiums you have encountered at the beginning of this piece. It happened as I left Monkey Island on my way to the party pavilion, overlooking the elephant compound. I was suddenly overtaken with great emotion and happiness that I was having such a good time with my husband in this little private, clean oasis. For the moment last Sunday morning, we were the only people at the top of the zoo before the playground began with its swings and space for active tots. I smelled the sweet air, marveled at the tiny primates, their curiosity and resemblance to man and felt this was indeed a magical time and place. All of a sudden everything noticeably brightened and an epiphany was upon me.

Let's discuss the meaning of epiphany. All the other writers who use this word never explain it and I always have to look it up, and then I never remember the next time I need it what the dictionary said. Here goes. Epiphany is explained by James Joyce as meaning a moment of spiritual manifestation, a most delicate and effervescent moment. Joyce himself in his late teens began to collect a notebook full of them, and collected approximately 70 for use in his later novels. These sudden and unanticipated moments of spiritual manifestation are used rather like prose poems set into the narrative structure of Joyce's work. The epiphany is significant also for the evocation of an already existing, but undefined, interior state. I prefer to have my epiphanies in private gardens or wilderness spaces myself, and the surrounds of this moment unleash a flood of half-happy and half-painful tears. I was in real touch with the fact that I owed this beautiful moment to the closeness with my spouse and to nature, and the creatures we share our home with on this earth. I also could truly mourn for the fact that I had not had this as a child. I was not taken to the zoo or the circus, as I so longed to be by my parents. That hurt. But finally I have just what I want, closeness and acceptance of my priorities and feelings by somebody very important to me. I was not read to as a child at all either and had to discover the delights of Babar, Rin Tin Tin, not to mention Tin Tin and Winnie the Pooh as I bought them for and read them to my own children. The sadness of parents who were themselves so embattled and miserable that they did not and could not make a child happy swept over me. The many years of misery washed away and I was left calm and content at last, realizing that which I had lost, but sharing this current wonderful experience with the person I most wanted to. It is not wonderful alone. I nurtured this husband through far and remote times in our relationship, and have been rewarded with good enough living so that I can afford analysis, so that I can really enjoy my life and enhance both of our existences. Pretty neat I would say. The fact that it's taken almost thirty years is not the point, that it's happened at all is.

CIRCUMCISION

I haven't hit old age quite yet. I'll let you know when and if I do. I have a hunch that Medicare will run out just as soon as I get to that mythical—for too many souls—place in life. In the meantime, before I get old enough to find all the old issues flat and silly, I thought I would take one last look at circumcision. You see, I don't like it. A few years back, my grandbaby was just about to go under the *mohel's* knife (it's more like a cigar cutter). I decided it wasn't for me.

At first I was astonished by my own resistance to this supposedly salutary procedure—a hallowed ritual for Jews, of course. Then again, practices and beliefs in a free society naturally ebb and flow discreetly under, as well as above, its surface. Perfectly decent, conventional people give voice and flesh to new and different ideas in the privacy of their bedrooms or automobiles. Those new ideas gestate. For the same purpose, subgroups, violent or not, form in the vastness of Montana or the basements of Long Island.

Sometimes fear and displacement of hated parts of the self get attributed to these groups, which were actually, at their inception, quite innocent. Soon, anyone with a different color, texture or body build is suspect. So is anyone who eats different foods or chooses a different day of the week to worship. Or even a different time of day, or number of times per day, to pray. Until, that is, usually with time, what was previously anomalous is accepted and assimilated, if not adopted.

Anyway, I have just heard the most astonishing group of supposedly professional people unjustly shortcut a discussion which began to question circumcision.

Let's face it. Wastes accumulate, are excreted, and have to be cleaned up. For example, even the white stuff that accumulates in the corners of our eyes, (in some people much more so than in others, because of allergies or dust). To cure that, you'd have to cut your eyes out. What about anuses, those stinky rear ends of babies and other people? We could eviscerate them, right, just like a fishmonger does shrimp—he cuts out the black track, full of dirt, sand and filth.

Have you ever smelled a female after a few days? Or after she's excreted blood or whiffed just her plain, everyday secretions? The genital tissues of both genders excrete fluids; but that's because those tissues have to be moist to work! If you've seen ads for deodorants and panty-liners, you know that women are moist and they drip, never mind menstruation. So, is that a good reason to have a hysterectomy or some other curative operation? Some people think so in Africa, as do others here. But that's a tragic misconception—done on an involuntary basis, as circumcision is done, it would be barbarous. The tipoff that we're talking basically the same insanity in both cases is that, when you ask why the operations must be done, you hear "because it's always been done this way by our people."

People, wake up! Human beings are animals. If periodically we produce waste, the answer is periodic cleansing showers, baths, douches, wet washcloths. Not attempting to conceal the uncomfortable truth of our existence by zapping organs here and there.

I always relish the question that is asked me as my adversaries' final sally. "Well, yes, but have you ever seen an uncircumcised penis?"

"Sure," I say, it's not shocking or ugly to me. "They look the way they look." We're talking cutting a boy here, not trimming and shaping a French poodle. In circumcision, we're not even talking prudently and kindly reshaping a disfigurement, much less one that the subject has asked to be reshaped, as in the case of adult plastic surgery.

Mark my words, all of you; circumcision will soon be considered child abuse. Just look at how differently we treat older kids now than in days of yore. Everyone used to smack their kids into the next county when they were disobedient. A much larger proportion of parents now care how their kids will think of them when they as grown parents are much less willing to risk the manifold repercussions of corporal punishment.

I think the same may happen regarding the violence of circumcision. The knowledge that the odds have now changed, medically, against a disease process plaguing those who aren't circumcised, the function and place of this surgery could very well change.

Remember, circumcision is not a word, a prayer, and a song, friends. It's cutting into the flesh of one's baby for no good reason. Inevitably we all bear, consciously or unconsciously, the guilt and bad feelings of that fundamental transgression. Inflicting pain inevitably means a fracture of trust, the trust we prize with regard to ourselves as well as others. Yes, there is rarely serious infection, scarring, or other long-term damage, but the enterprise is self-damaging to us a group. If not sadistic then, at the very least, masochistic. We don't need enemies; we have parents and *mohels*.

Of course, there was little choice in my day. Both my sons were peeled of a band of skin around their penises on their fourth day in the hospital. No discussion back then: It was a medical, not a personal, decision. It never occurred to me, not once, to question this years ago. Only recently, when working with a friend in the Loma Linda hospital nursery, doing the Brazelton tests, did I have access to newborns on a weekly basis and things became clear.

I often saw five of them hung up on boards, strapped in, sort of like Indian babies on their backboards, only they had been circumcised, and they were screaming in pain and agony. Red in the face. No one cared. Doctors and nurses went about their business. Yes, it was like being part of a Nazi medical experiment. To my anguished questions the answer always was, it's all right, they'll calm down, they'll get over it.

Medical literature suggests that babies do feel pain, although for years and years even pediatricians denied this. Not only did I not care for what was actually happening. I was also suspicious that the experienced medical personnel on hand were being conditioned to the babies' suffering. Like the allergists I've taken my kids to on occasion. They were seemingly impervious to the pain of the shots or tests—what was their explanation, it was necessary cause, it would save vastly more pain and illness later, the kids will calm down, they'll get used to it.

Okay, to save the considerable discomfort of allergies, but circumcision is largely a symbolic gesture, justified (marginally) with the rationale of mere "hygiene." I just can't handle such ritual mutilation.

WHOOPS, PARDON MY UNCONSCIOUS

After at least seven years during which I have been hoping my older son would settle down, it seems like my wish is about to come true, He's found a girl he seems to get along with more or less successfully, there are no major problems of any sort, furthermore she is highly eligible for the position of "the girlfriend."

This first son is the adventuresome one, and it has been quite a coup that he is still in one piece after many wild adventures, mostly climbing strange remote mountains and partying too much, too often, and with sometimes too enthusiastic friends.

There are a lot of bad things going on out there in the world. It is not so wonderful for singles, older singles anymore. The pendulum has swung toward commitment again and AIDS is nature's way of saying...get serious!

The present candidate for daughter-in-law is bright, athletic, and most of all can hold her own against all-too-opinionated young pup. She isn't even Thai, a Mau Mau princess, or a member of a revolutionary kamikaze squad. She's not into lacto-vegetarianism, nor does she consume products grown only on one unsprayed plot near Billings, Montana.

Wait, it gets even better. Last weekend Hubby and I schlepped up to San Francisco the hard way. We flew.

I had begged and begged a stubborn Hubby to please motor, his car or mine (he claims my Jag makes his back sore, I claim his driving makes my neurotransmitters sore.)

We went United. A word to the wise—don't. We could have gotten there faster walking. It took eight hours of endless waiting around the airport where strange travelers take out their anxieties by seeing how much cigarette smoke they can blow into your face per hour without my needing major cardio-pulmonary equipment. Strange kiddies throw up on your shoes from heat and exhaustion, and when the plane finally recovers from intensive care and starts moving, only four hours late for a fifty minute flight, airline personnel boom messages into your head non-stop at blast volume, my current pet peeve. I miss the good old days, when unless the plane was on fire or in a steep one way dive toward an oil refinery, you didn't hear about it. After paying an outrageous sum of money to travel a few hundred miles, the least one could expect would be some well-earned quiet, not commercials for their frequent flyer club. Delivered at rock concert pitch—the only way to get attention from rock concert- hardened audience?

Messes at the other end, rental cars not ready, Hertz travel buses and help-yourself portage giving one a hernia, all in all I am driving next time, whatever Hubby decides he wants to do. I may not be able to control covert operations in Central America, but I sure as hell can listen to the station I want to, and not be blasted out of my seat every three minutes with an unwelcome announcement.

And I can therewith ever decisively shake those shriekers, smokers and squirmers into the bargain.

Well, we arrive and good things start to happen. I think it's called maturity.

First-born son and "the girlfriend" actually treat us like company. We are looked for, cooked for, (very well, too) and booked for. Shown around to various friends. Introduced to relations. And entertained by senior partners.

All this is a big change from normal operating procedure, where we are greeted, meated, deleted. In other words, the kids usually come home, eat dinner then take off to be with their friends, which definitely do not include ole mom and dad.

But this weekend we are the guests. And we blossom into Mom and Dad. We get promoted. We are cased and upper-cased.

Something serious is going on. We are shown the local sights. There are lovely parts of Marin County no one would dream exist, out of the way, mostly army property, the loveliest in the city, as everyone knows. What everyone does not know, however, is about the bird sanctuary in the wetland area near the tower of the Golden Gate Bridge. And the Marine Mammal sanctuary close by, where volunteers cater to the orphans washed up on beaches and pups that've lost their mothers. Actually, one well-meaning tourist, thinking the mom is hard at work in the sea feeding herself and filling up with fresh fish to feed to junior upon her return. Misguided blanket put over pup caused her to suffocate. Benighted beachgoers kept the baby seal so warm that by the time they got him to the aquarium, he had suffered brain damage from the heat of blanket and car. Those waters are very cold indeed.

Sausalito is charming, hilly, and rustic. We view fireworks on the Fourth of July, likewise rustic. Puny compared with L.A. or San Diego, but who the heck cares?

Pictures of a friend's baby adorn the refrigerator and tables of the new little rented house high in the hills.

The writing's on the wall, folks. Settling down time. I really am tickled pink.

The only thing is, every time I start to address the charming young lady who is my son's choice, and with whom I first, nor last… fore nor sure, floats up. It's a total blank.

As we say in the business, Oedipus, Schmedipus, as long as you love your mother. In my case, your daughter-in-law to be.

Could it be I've been the only female amongst three males for too long? Don't want to give up the Queen Bee position, eh? Who would have thunk it, as grandpa Lou would have said.

NO NEED TO DIET

We drove in the rain, dreary and chill
Over bridges. thru tunnels and round and round hills
To experiment, with family, to try and see
What was this thing, molecular gastronomy?
This restaurant which cooked, a la Napa
But with no figs, but plenty of grappa
We each chose and assembled
Our three plates that resembled Nothing
ever seen before on this Earth. And
nothing that would add to our girth,
Another way to express the chef's way of dining
Is deconstructed: sort of throw things together you hope will be good.
And if you make a mistake, and nothing tastes like it should
Just skip the food, and go straight to the wining.
The sauces and gravies and herbs, oh my gosh.
My first son will love them, and his name is Josh.
Herbs and spices galore
They use more and more: mince of mint
frond of fennel
mousse of mushroom.
Pastiche of pistachio
The food, when it came, was delicious and hot
Portions were tiny, but prices were not.
A slice of sturgeon, with sea urchin emulsion A
squiggle of squid..... they use jet propulsion... A
slice of rare boeuf
On the plate with one carrot
A smidgeon of fowl
(Could it be a gray parrot?)
Would I go back again?

Well, here's how I think
If I want food that fractionated
I'd go right to the brink
Yes, I'd have my dinner at C.E.R.N., the l.h.c.
Where they have lots of P.h.D's To
REALLY really take things apart
And put back together, with ease
A cosmic plan that makes sense
And not just for folks with degrees.
I'd eat all I want, whatever I please
Knowing full well, in a couple of years
The more chubby people will have plenty to cheer
Because with the ever, exponentially expanding universe
We will all be taller and taller
And thinner and thinner
Beyond the blue people from Avatar.
And having some extra avoirdupois will be a survival advantage.
So Hardy HAR. HAR?

GOVERNERATOR

Bears
I like bears.
Teddy
Gummi
Cal bruins
Chicago bears
Polar Panda
Grizzly
Except for Arnold.
I don't
Think
Bears
Should govern
A big state like California
Do you?

NO BEGINNINGS

Time, tumbling down translucent transoms
Into the dark abyss of extinction.
Or: See: The trip ends in another scenario
Where time is not extinguished at all
A la ancient Mayan calendar
I Ching revelations other apocalyptic prognosis
But becomes flexible as chewed bubble gum
A veritable mobius strip Where
past, present and future Blur
together in a glorious NOW. No
beginnings—and even better No
endings
And
That will be
A great big WOW.

MICHELLE

Daughters Obama Go
home to your mama
There is no more drama
She's already met with the queen
They've hugged and they've kissed
Not a gesture was missed
And they both are supposedly mean.
But the world's economy's shattered
Protocol hardly much matters
The two moms are free to embrace
It's no longer a question of race.
The end of the world
It may come, it may go
But with females in frocks
There's a fashion show!
Whether the Gap, or Givenchy Eddie Bauer or such
There's always reporters
To make much of a much.
So little Obamas, take heed of your mama
And spiff up those outfits right now
Whether left, right or center
Consult with your mentor
To guide your to beauty
You know, it's your duty
To be on the top,
In a world full of fops
It's not just street creds
You must have the coolest of threads.
Take care with your hair
Give it plenty of flair
The right shape color and style

Will earn you plenty of smiles
Paparazzi have passion
For color! For fashion!
So assemble those ensembles
In size misses, pluses or tall
Let's eye that clothing
And see the effect overall
Duds from Old Navy
Cardigans from J. Crew
Michelle and girls
It's all up to you.
To make some big slashes
At international bashes To
out couture the Frogs And
other European snobs Who
think that their dresses Can
outguess the Guesses. So
take up the reins
With those looks and those brains
Though Carla is cool She did
not go to school Neither
Oxford nor Cambridge She
couldn't do what you did. (She
did look very demure
In her Christian Dior.)
The polls are all in—An American win!
So let's hear a holler
For wife, mom and scholar
Whose clothes off the rack
Took the whole world aback.
Well, Michelle's so chi-chi
We'll have to wait and see
If the first ladies' habille Will triumph consistently.
P.S.
A cheer for Obama
And happy transition To
your exalted position Of
first Pup.

SWITCH

Jung said it, Freud read it. Abet it? Regret it!
What? Oh, I get it.
It.: that tastes never would change.
The notion, by gum
and by golly.
That weird as it
strange as it
deranged as it
strikes you
At mid-point
the mid-life
phase.
When couples briefly
slyly
Pass and Yikes!
Astoundingly blithely
SWITC<u>*H*</u> positions in
Regard to
In view of In
spite of
Former tastes
In temperatures, climates
Degrees of either Celsius
or Fahrenheit.
Comfort zones turn suddenly crazily
UNCOMFORTABLE.
To be brief, and in short.
Turnabout, upside down, Benedict Arnold sort
of Traitorous, puzzling weird sort of SWITCH.
I used to be

EXOTIC EPIPHANIES

Since age of three a
Shivery, chill-brained sort.
Infernally cool
at home or in school.
When others were toasty
and roasty
as a rule.
My blood did cool
to a different drummer. It was hell.
I shivered, I shook and my lips turned pale blue.
Especially when hit by a draft
I bundled right up like Nanook of the North.
It was cruel.
Then along about fifty my
body changed—Nifty!
I burned like an oven a-blast.
To the query, is anyone else feeling hot in this room?
The answer came back very fast.
Not at all, not at all.
And I asked for a few years until
I have finally amassed Evidence
for my rule
That:
If you were the one to get up at night and sneak the thermostat
up three notches when Hubby, last time he was conscious, said
"it's stifling in here already." Then you can be sure, once
you're both on the shady side of forty—and the sunny side
of sixty.
That someone will creep out of bed to turn it down.
And the one, formerly sunk up to his earlobes in covers never
minding any conditions once he is asleep
Will be creeping out to the hall controls and trying to warm up
the place.
After which the other formerly gelid one
will silently slip open the sliding glass door
A crack or three
To avoid that most unpleasant condition
Of being parboiled
by dawn.

It's an anomaly, mystery, heresay
worse than transsexual change
To have the hot one turn cold
And vice-versa, I'm told
Gives a brand new meaning
to mid-life "derange."
But stop! Wait! Hold! Tarry!
Take care when you marry.
And do not your opposite find
Of course he must be he
and a she stays a she
But all other qualities should combine
So that mix, mate or match
when it comes down to scratch
At the end, all in all, you won't mind.
If formerly you both loved to sleep with blizzards gusting
through the bedclothes,
By mid-life, I guarantee you, you'll both be able to raise
African violets in the boudoir. And that, dear ones, is how to
stay out of divorce court, I find.
As for us, we limp on,
Always hoping, some morn
That L.A. will resume its best trick
of remaining so fair
There is need for no air
Save the natural breezes that blow
Right now it's all moot
For in truth and in ruth
Our heater's broken down with a clang
One of us is wearing socks, scarves and gloves to bed
the other's in batiste and organdy.
Guess which is which... go ahead.

TRUE GREEN

Envious of emeralds
Full of greedy glee
When I see the 40 karat sparklers worn by Angelina Jolie
I COULD JUST EXPIRE WITH PURE ENVY
If I were tall and gorgeous
Just like Angelina Jolie
And wore 5 inch stilettos on my feet
And threw off that much heat
I'd buy those gems in one heartbeat
But being rather shortish From
my head down to my feet That are
clad in comfy Ugg boots
3/4 of the year well glamour's out for me
Because I'm happy in my Uggs
And I fear I may get mugged
Without an entourage and cheering fans to protect me
I'll keep the two-page color spread
Safely hung above the bed.
And keep the thieves and robbers at bay.
And "have" them always on display.

THAT WAS DINNER?

We drove in the rain, dreary and chill
Over the bridges, thru tunnels and round and round hills
To experiment, with family, to try and see
What was this thing, molecular gastronomy?
This restaurant which cooked, a la Napa
But with no figs, but plenty of grappa
We each chose and assembled Our
three plates that resembled Nothing
ever seen before on this earth.
And nothing that would add to our girth
Another way to express the chef's way of dining
Is deconstructed: sort of throw things together you hope will be good
And if you make a mistake, and nothing tastes like it should
Just skip the food, and go straight to the wining.
The sauces and gravies and herbs, oh my gosh.
My first son will love them, and his name is Josh.
Herbs and spices galore
They use more and more:
Mince of mint
Frond of fennel
Mousse of mushroom
Tartin of truffle
A scintilla of cinnamon
Garnish of young garlic
Pastiche of pistachio
The food, when it came, was delicious and hot
Portions were tiny but prices were not.
A slice of sturgeon, with sea urchin emulsion A squiggle
of squid.....they use jet propulsion A slice of rare boeuf

On the plate with one carrot
A smidgeon of fowl
(Could it be a gray parrot?)
Would I go back again? Well, here's how I think
If I want food that fractionated
I'd go right to the brink
Yes, I'd have my dinner at Large Hadron Collider
Where they have lots of P.H.D.'s To
REALLY really take things apart
And put back together, with ease
A cosmic plan that makes sense
And not just for folks with advanced degrees.
I'd eat all I want, whatever I please
Knowing full well, in a couple of years
The more chubby people we'll have plenty to cheer Because with
the ever, exponentially expanding universe With planets and
galaxies speeding away from each other And thinner and thinner
And cooler and cooler
Beyond the blue people of Avatar.
And having some extra avoirdupois will be a survival advantage.
Before the final spaghetti-zation
So Hardy Har Har?

NO MORE TWEET OR TWITTER

I never had trouble communicating
I could read, I could write, I could spell
And I took typing at Penn State
To ensure I could do them all well
I thought this would be all I'd ever need
To bring me, and keep me, up to speed.
Humpff!
All the new devices and their updates
Obsolescing in just days
Leave me numb
I never considered myself dumb
Mechanical skills I surely lack
New inventions take me a-back.
No blue, black or straw
Berries for me
No smart phone, dumb phone
No blockbuster, 4G or WiFi technology
No IPads, IPod, you-pads, me-pads Don't
want no virtual "meet" or "pow-wow" Surely
I've met enough people by now?
No apps, facebook, Im's, sky-skype
Don't want to hear about all that hype
I don't want to befriend any more folks
For this grandma that's a big joke
Just want to use my good old land-line phone
And talk to my own OLD friends all alone
I don't want to scan or stencil
I'm back to using paper, pencil
I want to be left in situ

To write a haiku or two
So bah and phooey to all the flurry
Let the information tsunami roll, I'm in no hurry
I don't want to tweet
I don't want to twitter
Just want to sit here—old and bitter.

BRAIN

With added megabytes of memory for the I-pad and other
Gadgets, do-dads and robotic brains
My memory's slipping—done gone down de drain!
Is outsourcing one's I. Q. really a gain? Might
we not need to access it sometime again?

I LEARNED IT AT CAL TECH

There was a young man from Peking Who
did some very deep profound thinking This
man by the name of Yao
Found a teensy particle some how
A trillionth the size of an electron
We won't be able to verify his calculations for n
No technology exists for this super-duper micro world
Not even remotely qualified
To make any statement to prove or disprove this theory;
I am positively defunct in the non-verbal dimensions
(I never got the same answer twice
In second grade math.)
I still don't!

These Yao manifolds come under Aegis
Of string theory
Which is not thought of as being nearly so
Mathematically correct as quantum mechanics
Which has been repeatedly measured
To be accurate to one part in ten billion
Making it the most successful physical theory of all time.

Scientists mostly, male
Trying to understand
The nature of matter at its smallest scale:
Quantum mechanics

Particle physics;
The atom bomb

The neutron bomb
The particle bomb
But now there are gluons and muons
And don't give a hoo-on
And did you know the heaviest particle ever found?
Is its quark bound up with its anti-quark?

Also a lepton as well as its anti-particle
Equals the Tau Lepton
It is VERY heavy

I thought we were down to the limit
With science right up to the minute

I wonder what about the very elusive Higgs particle
That is supposed, like molasses
To provide mass to the empty space that
Makes up the structure of the cosmos.

BIO

Elinor Floum is a new freelance author, treading the artistic continuum between "budding" and "overblown." Not as fresh as Alice Kahn, nor as worldly-wise as Erma Bombeck, she nevertheless hopes to have something of interest to say to the semi-conscious. Neither baby-boomer nor quite yet senior citizen...except, for all practical purposes, at the AMC Cineplex 14, where she can frequently be seen hustling her Reeboks, for half prices-natch-into a flick or three.

What in the world is this book about? If anything, besides an exercise in narcissism?

Well really, it should be called "sessions off the couch." The original intent was to have a "session" when on vacation; in some other words, to mentally talk to my analyst, to process experience, to free associate. To get in touch with my deepest thoughts, to "make overt what is covert," which I thought would be beneficial. A diary of my sessions and to myself. How do I know what I am thinking till I put it down in writing?

Answer: I don't. Lessons from Jung: paint, sing, write, do something to let it all out, and let the conscious mind then add input from the subconscious new meaning. Et Voila.

Me-addressing other and unknown parts of the self. See, unlike Ionesco, I don't need six other characters to dialogue with; I am split into so many fragments so I can just talk to myself and have a fairly hefty cast of people interacting.

A vacation from an analyst, yes. But not vacation from analysis. Or from sessions with myself.

www.ingramcontent.com/pod-product-compliance
Lightning Source LLC
Chambersburg PA
CBHW030339310726
48979CB00001B/100
9780983340294